DISCUSSION PAPER 59

THE ZIMBABWEAN NATION-STATE PROJECT

A Historical Diagnosis of Identity and Power-Based Conflicts in a Postcolonial State

SABELO J. NDLOVO-GATSHENI

NORDISKA AFRIKAINSTITUTET, UPPSALA 2011

Indexing terms:
Zimbabwe
Nationalism
State
Political conflicts
Political development
Political leadership
Elite
Ethnicity
National identity
Nation-building
Post-colonialism

The opinions expressed in this volume are those of the author and do not necessarily reflect the views of Nordiska Afrikainstitutet.

Language checking: Peter Colenbrander

ISSN 1104-8417

ISBN 978-91-7106-696-1

Production: Byrå4

Print on demand, Lightning Source UK Ltd.

Contents

Acknowledgements

I express my thanks to the anonymous reviewers for carefully reading the draft manuscript and coming up with useful comments that helped me sharpen my analysis. I also owe special thanks to Cyril Obi of the Nordic Africa Institute for commissioning this study and for shepherding the process of its writing from conception to publication.

List of Acronyms

ANC	African National Council
ANC-S	African National Council-Sithole
ANC-Z	African National Council-Zimbabwe
DRC	Democratic Republic of Congo
ESAP	Economic Structural Adjustment Programme
FROLIZI	Front for the Liberation of Zimbabwe
GPA	Global Political Agreement
IG	Inclusive Government
IMF	International Monetary Fund
MDC	Movement for Democratic Change
MHS	Matabele Home Society
MMD	Movement for Multiparty Democracy
NAI	Nordic Africa Institute
NAM	Non-Aligned Movement
NDP	National Democratic Party
NDR	National Democratic Revolution
NGOs	Non-Governmental Organisations
OAU	Organisation of African Unity
PF-ZAPU	Patriotic Front-Zimbabwe African Peoples Union
PM	People's Movement
SADC	Southern African Development Community
SRANC	Southern Rhodesia African National Congress
UANC	United African National Council
UDI	Unilateral Declaration of Independence
UN	United Nations
ZANLA	Zimbabwe African National Liberation Army
ZANU	Zimbabwe African National Union
ZANU-PF	Zimbabwe African National Union-Patriotic Front
ZAPU	Zimbabwe African People's Union
ZARU	Zimbabwe African Regional Union
ZATU	Zimbabwe African Tribal Union
ZCTU	Zimbabwe Congress of Trade Unions
ZINASU	Zimbabwe National Students Union
ZIPA	Zimbabwe People's Army
ZIPRA	Zimbabwe People's Revolutionary Army
ZLC	Zimbabwe Liberation Committee
ZNP	Zimbabwe National Party

Foreword

This Discussion Paper provides an insightful, historically-rooted analysis of the crisis of the nation-state project in Africa, based on a case study of Zimbabwe. In this regard, it addresses issues related to the evolution of the Zimbabwe national project against the background of resistance to settler colonialism; the contradictions that attended the nationalist struggle, particularly the divisions along the lines of race and the less-focused issues of ethnicity, personality and ideological difference; and the postcolonial challenges to the nation-state project. These latter include the project's betrayal by some of its heroes; its undermining by the increased power of international institutions and forces of globalisation in a post-Cold war world; economic crises; and generational changes. The paper posits that the nation-state project on the continent is very much a work-in-progress and is faced with many challenges.

The Zimbabwe case study examines the roots of the crisis of nation-statism by critically examining the nature of the colonial state as a racialised bifurcated structure, within which ethnic fault-lines emerged, contributing to the fragmentation of nationalist and liberation movements. It also describes in great detail the personality differences within the nationalist elite, the leadership struggles and the use of ethnicity to account for some of the divisions within the liberation movements. The author provides a radical analysis that locates the Zimbabwean question within the crucial challenge of forming and constructing a common national identity and citizenship out of different races and ethnic groups and in the shadow of the country's troubled past.

Of note is the observation that the Lancaster House Agreement, largely dominated by the UK and US, was largely responsible for compromising a 'revolutionary transition' that could have resolved the racially biased inequalities in land and asset distribution in postcolonial Zimbabwe. However, the Zimbabwean postcolonial nationalist elite are not let off lightly. Indeed their role in the crisis described as a 'revolution that lost its way' is brought under close scrutiny. The author points out that the National Democratic Revolution (NDR) was vague on issues of democracy, social justice and human rights. He goes on to note how the nation-state project has progressively regressed since 2000 as a result of several emerging trends: an 'imperial' presidency; increased state coercion and repression of opposition; shrinkage of the democratic space; and the emergence of war veterans as a pro-government force.

The paper undertakes a critique of post-2000 developments in Zimbabwe, particularly the struggles between the ZANU-PF government and the opposition MDC. Noteworthy is the critique of the Global Political Agreement (GPA) and the contradictions within ZANU-PF and its quest to continue to define the Zimbabwe nation-state project. The paper concludes by examining the challenges facing a beleaguered nationalist leadership responding to crisis with repression and largely militarised institutions in an international context dominated by neoliberal forces.

This paper is of key importance to scholars, decision-makers and activists with a deep interest in Zimbabwe and the broader nation-state project in Africa.

Cyril Obi
Senior Researcher
The Nordic Africa Institute

1. Introduction

> *[A]t the heart of the modern nation-state project was the idea, flawed from the outset, of a tight correspondence between the nation and the state whereby each sovereign state was seen as a nation-state of people who shared a common language or culture ... This notion of the nation-state stood in direct contradiction to the reality that most states were, in fact, multi-cultural and multi-religious and that not all ethnic groups (however defined) were sufficiently large or powerful or even willing to achieve a state of their own.*
>
> —Liisa Laakso and Adebayo O. Olukoshi[1]

> *A spectre is haunting Zimbabwe – the spectre of racialised dispossession ... Postcolonial Zimbabwe remained haunted by entanglements of race, rule and land rights.*
>
> —Donald S. Moore[2]

> *The 'nation' should have the 'right' to self-determination. But who is that 'nation' and who has the authority and the 'right' to speak for the 'nation' and express its will? How can we find out what the 'nation' actually wants? Does there exist one political party which would not claim that it alone, among all others, truly expresses the will of the 'nation' whereas all other parties give only perverted and false expressions of the national will?*
>
> —Rosa Luxemburg[3]

Nationalism defined as the process of identity-making can be well understood in the words of Stephen Reicher and Nick Hopkins as 'the best of beliefs and ... the worst of beliefs.'[4] This understanding of nationalism is further amplified by a British Labour politician who likened nationalism to electricity that can be used for good and bad purposes. He continued that 'it can electrocute someone in the electric chair or it can heat and light the world,' adding that:

> Nationalism can be an exhilarating revolutionary force for progress ... But we only have to open our newspapers today to areas where nationalism becomes in the wrong hands a primeval force of darkness and reaction ... I can say cynically, we ought to utilise the potential revolutionary force of nationalism and by our leadership, ensure that the dark side of the beast does not emerge.[5]

1. L. Laakso and A.O. Olukoshi, 'The Crisis of the Post-Colonial Nation-State Project in Africa,' in A. O. Olukoshi and L. Laakso (eds), *Challenges to the Nation-State in Africa* (Uppsala: Nordic Africa Institute, 1996), pp. 11–12.
2. D.S. Moore, *Suffering for Territory: Race, Place, and Power in Zimbabwe* (Harare: Weaver Press, 2005), p. ix.
3. R. Luxemburg, *The National Question* (New York: Monthly Review, 1976), p. 141.
4. S. Reicher and N. Hopkins, *Self and Nation: Categorisation, Contestation and Mobilisation* (London: Sage Publications, 2001), p. 53.
5. Quoted in Reicher and Hopkins, *Self and Nation*, pp. 56–7.

If nationalism is mobilised for progressive purposes, it leads to the formation of national identity within a political institution called the state. It has the potential to make both the state (making of nation-as-state) and nation (making of nation-as-people). Kwesi Kaa Prah provides a positive definition of African nationalism:

> African nationalism is a modernist response of Africans to the political, social, economic and cultural depredations of (particularly) Western overlordship. It is African self-assertiveness in the face of the contradictions of Western encroachment, subjugation, imposition and rule not only in the political sense, but also in the socio-psychological, social, cultural and economic dimensions of social life. It is modernist in the sense that it is a reaction which has benefited from the leadership of Western-educated Africans and advised by contemporary, universally subscribed, ideas of freedom and emancipation.[6]

Any nation-state project refers to that protean process of making the nation-as-state and making the nation-as-people. Ideally, a good political community is one whose citizens are actively engaged in deciding their common future together. Bound together by ties of national solidarity, they discover and implement principles of justice that all can share, and in doing so they respect the separate identities of minority groups within the community.[7] In reality, however, as noted by Michael Billig, the creation of the 'nation-as-people' has never been a harmonious process by which, for example, a traditional 'ethnie' grows from 'small shoot into the full flower of nationality, as if following a process of "natural" maturation.' The process is typically attended by conflict and violence. 'A particular form of identity has to be imposed. One way of thinking of the self, of community and, indeed of the world has to replace other conceptions, other forms of life.'[8] This process is even more complicated in ex-colonies where imperialism and colonialism added the politics of race to the equally complex layers of the 'tribe,' ethnicity, religion and regionalism and other power struggles emanating from pre-colonial histories.

Worse still, as African nation-builders (African nationalist leaders/founding fathers of postcolonial states) were engaged in the highly sensitive and delicate project of making the 'nation-as-state' (state-making) and 'nation-as-people' (nation-building), they had to navigate complex global politics fashioned by such processes as the Cold War and the global wave of neoliberalism that had a fragmenting impact on young African states. Liisa Laakso and Adebayo Olu-

---

6. K.K. Prah, 'A Pan-Africanist Reflection: Point and Counterpoint,' (Unpublished Paper, Centre for Advanced Studies of African Society (CASAS), University of Cape Town, 2009), p. 2.
7. D. Miller, *Citizenship and National Identity* (Cambridge: Polity Press, 2000).
8. M. Billig, *Banal Nationalism* (London: Sage Publications, 1995), p. 27.

koshi have noted that in Africa, ethnic and racial cleansing have combined with acute religious extremism, intolerance or pure criminality to suggest a growing social crisis in the international system. They concluded that:

> At the heart of this turmoil is the crisis of individual and group identity which, in the context of deepening social inequality/fragmentation, the weakened administrative and policy apparatuses of the state, the decline of ideologies of communism and anti-communism that dominated the Cold War years, and an accelerating process of globalisation, has called into question some of the basic premises of the contemporary nation-state project.[9]

The African national project, defined as that complex process of making of 'the African people' in the context of the struggle against colonialism and imperialism into a sovereign common collectivity in pursuit of cultural and political ends in general, and the Zimbabwean national project, defined as the 'conquest of conquest' (black natives conquering white settlers) through a series of *Chimurengas/Zvimurenga* (nationalist revolutions) culminating in the making of Zimbabwean national identity, are related processes, one macro and the other micro. Robert Mugabe described the Zimbabwean nation-state project in these words:

> We are now talking of conquest of conquest, the prevailing sovereignty of the people of Zimbabwe over settler minority rule and all it stood for including the possession of our land ... Power to the people must now be followed by land to the people.[10]

This is the popular definition of the Zimbabwean nation-state project as enunciated by Mugabe and ZANU-PF towards the beginning of 2000s. It was fully embraced by war veterans and others who still believed in the revolutionary character of ZANU-PF as a former liberation movement. But it was contested by the opposition and the civil society organisations that decried its racial undertones, its antipathy towards democracy and its disdain for human rights.

What is clear, however, is that a people called 'Zimbabweans' were a product of the nationalist struggle rather than a pre-colonial or primordial identity. Ivor Chipkin argued that African people as a collectivity organised in pursuit of a common cultural and political end did not precede the African nationalist struggle. Rather, an African 'people' came into being in the first place as a political collectivity in the midst of resistance to colonialism. He added that the

9. L. Laakso and A.O. Olukoshi, 'The Crisis of the Post-Colonial Nation – State Project in Africa,' in A.O. Olukoshi and L. Laakso (eds), *Challenges to the Nation-State in Africa* (Uppsala: Nordic Africa Institute, 1996), p. 20.
10. *The Herald*, 6 December 1997. See also S.J. Ndlovu-Gatsheni, 'The Nativist Revolution and Development Conundrums in Zimbabwe,' in *ACCORD Occasional Paper Series*, 1 (4) (2006).

nation is a political community whose form is given in relation to the pursuit of democracy and freedom. To him, the nation preceded the state, 'not because it has always existed, but because it emerges in and through the nationalist struggle for state power.'[11]

Highlighting the centrality of race and class within the African national project, Peter Ekeh argued that the African struggle for independence was nothing other than 'a struggle for power between the two bourgeois classes involved in the colonisation of Africa,' namely the entrenched white colonial bourgeoisie and the emerging black bourgeoisie.[12] The emerging African/black bourgeois was involved in the colonisation project through the creation of mission and colonial schools and churches, which uneasily straddled the white world students were taught to like and the African world they were told to belittle. Understood in this context, the African liberation struggle could not avoid assuming the form of a civil war between the black 'natives' and the white 'settlers,' making the liberation war in Zimbabwe take the form of an identity-based-conflict in which black 'natives' fought to defeat white 'settlers.'

To Kuan-Hsing Chen this was inevitable: 'Shaped by the immanence of colonialism, Third World nationalism could not escape from reproducing racial and ethnic discrimination; a price to be paid by the coloniser as well as the colonised selves.'[13] While it remains contestable whether it was really inevitable for African nationalism to reproduce ethnic and racial discrimination after the end of direct colonialism, there is no doubt that African nationalism was terribly and deeply interpellated by categories of colonialism. What is also clear is that on top of the race layer as a conflict-generating phenomenon was the problem of ethnicity, which was deliberately politicised by the colonial state as it denied African identities the chance to coalesce into a single national identity through rigid ethnic demarcations, legislative codifications (identity cards), census mappings and other cartographic measures that organised Africans into various ethnic groupings.

The imperatives of ethnicity, in combination with other factors such as ideological differences and personality clashes among leading nationalist actors, saw the Zimbabwean nationalist movements fragment into various factions. While historical research has focused on the ZAPU/ZIPRA and ZANU/ZANLA dichotomies, it has tended to ignore other factions, such as those led by Bishop Abel Muzorewa and Reverend Ndabaningi Sithole that eventually negotiated an 'internal settlement' with the Rhodesia leader Ian Smith in 1978, which culmi-

11. I. Chipkin, *Do South African Exist? Nationalism, Democracy and the Identity of 'the People,'* (Johannesburg: Wits University Press, 2007), pp. 1–14.
12. P. Ekeh, 'Colonialism and the Two Publics in Africa: A Theoretical Statement,' in *Comparative Studies in Society ad History*, 17 (1) (1975), p. 102.
13. K.H. Chen, 'Introduction: The Decolonisation Question,' in K.H. Chen (ed.), *Trajectories: Inter-Asia Cultural Studies* (London: Routledge, 1998), p. 14.

nated in the short-lived 'Zimbabwe-Rhodesia' government led by Bishop Muzorewa.[14] More often than not, those scholars who celebrated African nationalism and decolonisation as successful projects ignored the crucial antinomies in black liberation thought that translated into different visions, versions and imaginations of the postcolonial state, nation, citizenship and modes of rule.[15]

Looked at from the international perspective, the decolonisation process in Africa launched into international politics 'sovereign' postcolonial states as a 'group of the world's poorest, weakest, and most artificial states.'[16] One needs to add though that African states have never been a homogenous set of political entities suffering from the common problems that Christopher Clapham wanted us to accept. They ranged widely from those with very deep roots in a long tradition and history of existence as autonomous formations, like Egypt, to the most artificial states, like Somalia, which has collapsed in recent years. Thus, Robert H. Jackson's description of postcolonial states as 'quasi-states,' that is, states recognised as sovereign and independent units by other states within the international system, is also too much of a generalisation. While some postcolonial states could not meet the demands of 'empirical statehood,' which required the capacity to exercise effective power within their own territories and the ability to defend themselves effectively against external attack, others met the criteria in varying degrees.[17]

But the problem of the 'quasi-ness' of the majority of postcolonial states continues to haunt various African national projects, which remain a 'work-in-progress' aimed at carving out a niche in global politics and determining the state's own destiny as well as formulating its own African-oriented policies. As underpinned by various versions of nationalism, African national projects were never homogenous in reflecting and involving concrete struggles over material resources and moral possibilities.[18] I provide a detailed definition of the African national project in the next section of this study.

This study seeks to provide a historically-rooted interrogation of the Zimbabwean nation-state project. The main analytical focus is on how issues of

14. For instance N. Bhebe's *The ZAPU and ZANU Guerrilla Warfare and the Evangelical Lutheran Church in Zimbabwe* (Gweru: Mambo Press, 1999) ignores the other factions within the nationalist movements and concentrated on ZAPU and ZANU as though there were the only forces fighting for decolonisation in Rhodesia.
15. S.J. Ndlovu-Gatsheni, 'Black Republican Tradition, Nativism and Populist Politics in South Africa,' in *Transformation: Critical Perspectives on Southern Africa,* 68 (2008), pp. 53–86.
16. C. Clapham, *Africa and the International System: The Politics of State Survival* (Cambridge: Cambridge University Press, 1996).
17. R.H. Jackson, *Quasi-States: Sovereignty, International Relations and the Third World* (Cambridge: Cambridge University Press, 1990).
18. P.T. Zeleza, *Rethinking Africa's 'Globalisation' Volume 1: The Intellectual Challenges* (Trenton NJ: Africa World Press, 2003).

race, ethnicity, class, regionalism, generation and differential resource ownership mediated by the controllers of state power continue to generate conflict in Zimbabwe. I present a number of broad arguments in this paper.

The first is that the Zimbabwean nation-state project cannot be understood outside the broader African national project that unfolded after the end of the Second World War, culminating in the proliferation of independent postcolonial states from the 1960s onwards. The Zimbabwean national project is affected by the tribulations, crises and problems that continue to affect the broader African national project.

The second proposition is that those scholars who analysed the Zimbabwean national project in the 1980s during its triumphal phase produced 'praise-texts' and became willing scribes of the official meta-narrative. This narrative celebrated the independence struggle and in the process glossed over the epistemological limits, ideological poverty and realities of the Zimbabwean nationalist struggle as an avenue for the retribalisation of politics, as the key nationalist actors competed for dominance through ethnic mobilisation. Commenting on how some of those who embraced the title 'nationalist' were in reality 'tribalists,' Jonathan Moyo wrote: 'Equally compelling was Msika's nationalism. Many have been called nationalists, but their record is a mixed tale of tribalism. Not Msika; he was not a lip-service nationalist who takes on a national character when there is a crowd before him.'[19] Praise texts produced by historians like Terence Ranger and Ngwabi Bhebe, journalists like David Martin and Phyllis Johnson, as well as anthropologists like David Lun, ignored the deep-seated scourge of tribalism that haunted the Zimbabwean nationalist project before and after 1980.[20]

The third proposition is that the often celebrated Zimbabwean nationalist struggle only succeeded in creating the 'nation-as-state' but failed dismally to create the 'nation-as-people.'[21]

---

19. J. Moyo, 'Man of Truth: The Late Vice President Joseph Msika,' in http://www.newzimbabwe.com/blog/?p=665. Moyo was locating the late vice president of Zimbabwe, Joseph Msika, at the centre of the nationalist struggle that was troubled by the deep-seated scourge of tribalism.

20. The idea of praise text is borrowed from S. Robin, 'Heroes, Heretics and Historians of the Zimbabwe Revolution: A Review Article of Norma Kriger's "Peasant Voices" (1992),' in *Zambezia*, XXIII (i) (1996), p. 74. For examples of praise text, see T. Ranger, *Peasant Consciousness and Guerrilla War in Zimbabwe* (Harare: Zimbabwe Publishing House, 1985); D. Martin and P. Johnson, *The Struggle for Zimbabwe: The Chimurenga War* (Harare: Zimbabwe Publishing House, 1981); D. Lun, *Guns and Rain: Guerrillas and Spirit Mediums in Zimbabwe* (Harare: Zimbabwe Publishing House, 1985); and N. Bhebe, *The ZAPU and ZANU Guerrilla Warfare and the Evangelical Lutheran Church in Zimbabwe* (Gweru: Mambo Press, 1999) and N. Bhebe, *Simon Vengayi Muzenda and the Struggle for and Liberation of Zimbabwe* (Gweru: Mambo Press, 2004).

21. S.J. Ndlovu-Gatsheni, *Do 'Zimbabweans' Exist? Trajectories of Nationalism, National Identity Formation and Crisis in a Postcolonial State* (Oxford: Peter Lang AG International Academic Publishers, 2009–in press).

Finally, I argue that the crisis that engulfed Zimbabwe at the beginning of the third millennium has its deep roots in the legacies of settler colonialism and the inherent limits of African nationalism. This reality has far-reaching implications for the shape of Zimbabwe's nation-state project. In the first place, control over and access to land has continued to shape and influence postcolonial political contestations and imaginations of freedom, because 'control over land and production on it became a crucial aim of the Southern Rhodesia administration and governments.'[22] Blair Rutherford noted that land in Zimbabwe became associated with the nation; the national liberation struggle came to be interpreted as a peasant struggle for land; and the political rhetoric of ZANU-PF as well as its policy prescriptions were formulated around the agrarian question.[23] The land and race question has formed the centrepiece of ZANU-PF's definition of belonging, citizenship, exclusion and the whole history of the nation. This was articulated clearly by President Robert Mugabe in these words:

> We knew and still know that land was the prime goal of King Lobengula as he fought British encroachment in 1893; we knew and still know that land was the principal grievance for our heroes of the First Chimurenga led by Nehanda and Kaguvi. We knew and still know it to be the fundamental premise of the Second Chimurenga and thus a principal definer of [the] succeeding new Nation and State of Zimbabwe. Indeed we know it to be the core issue of the Third Chimurenga which you and me are fighting, and for which we continue to make such enormous sacrifices.[24]

Even political contestation between ZANU-PF and the MDC did not escape implications of race. For example, Mugabe forcefully tried to delegitimise the MDC as nothing other than a front for white colonial interests. This is how he framed the MDC:

> The MDC should never be judged or characterised by its black trade union face; by its youthful student face; by its salaried black suburban junior professionals; never by its rough and violent high-density lumpen elements. It is much deeper than these human superficies; for it is immovably and implacably moored in the colonial yesteryear and embraces wittingly or unwittingly the repulsive ideology of return to white settler rule. MDC is as old and as strong as the forces that control it; that drive and direct; indeed that support, sponsor and spot it. It is a

22. B. Rutherford, 'Shifting Grounds in Zimbabwe: Citizenship and Farm Workers in the New Politics of Land, in S. Dorman, D. Hammett and P. Nugent (eds), *Making Nations, Creating Strangers: State and Citizenship in Africa* (Leiden and Boston: Brill, 2007), p. 106.
23. Ibid., p. 110. See also B. Rutherford, *Working on the Margins: Black Workers, White Farmers in Postcolonial Zimbabwe* (London and Harare: Zed and Weaver Press, 2001).
24. R.G. Mugabe, *Inside the Third Chimurenga* (Harare: Government of Zimbabwe, 2001), pp. 92–3.

> counter revolutionary Trojan horse contrived and nurtured by the very inimical forces that enslaved and oppressed our people yesterday.[25]

This situation has led Brian Raftopoulos to argue that one of the key features of the Zimbabwean crisis as it unfolded during the early 2000s was the emergence of a revived nationalism that was delivered in a particularly virulent form with race as its main trope.[26]

The study is organised into eight broad sections. The first section is this introduction, which defines the key issues examined throughout. The second examines the broad African national project as a framework within which the Zimbabwean nation-state project can be understood. In the third section, the historical background to the crisis of the nation-state in Zimbabwe is examined, particularly the racial and ethnic complexion that is proving hard to fashion into a common national identity and single citizenship. The fourth section analyses the long, difficult road to becoming national by examining the key nationalist political parties and their imagination of liberation and nationhood, including the inter-and intra-nationalist factionalisms and disunities of the 1960s and 1970s. The analysis of the nationalist visions of two key nationalist actors, the Reverend Ndabaningi Sithole and Bishop Abel Muzorewa, who have been written out of Zimbabwean political history and the struggle for national independence, forms the focus of section five.

This is followed by a critical examination of the transition politics in Zimbabwe, beginning with the Lancaster House Constitutional Conference and its failure to resolve the land question as a source of conflict and how ZANU-PF made strategic errors in its pursuit of the National Democratic Revolution. NDR remained vaguely defined in terms of removal of settler colonialism, reclamation of land and the introduction of 'one man, one vote.' When some of the nationalists in ZAPU and ZANU imbibed Marxist-Leninist-Maoist radical ideologies in the 1970s, the socialist/communist thought remained subordinated to the imperative of African nationalism. ZAPU and ZANU never matured into full-fledged communist organisations in the mould of the South African Communist Party (SACP), for instance. Owen Tshabangu concluded that ZAPU and ZANU, as bourgeois nationalist parties, comprised 'all and sundry' members, 'with their only qualification being that they say they subscribe to the demand for independence.' He added:

> All the party is interested in is quantity, not necessarily quality. The party wants an outward appearance of strength which may mask an internal weakness be-

25. Ibid, p. 88.
26. B. Raftopoulos, 'Nation, Race and History in Zimbabwean Politics,' in S. Dorman, D. Hammett and P. Nugent (eds), *Making Nations, Creating Strangers: States and Citizenship in Africa* (Leiden and Boston: Brill, 2007), p. 181.

> cause of the existence of various contradictory trends within, which usually come into the open during periods of stress – which quickly reveal themselves during such periods.[27]

This character of the nationalist movement helps to explain some of the political and strategic mistakes of ZANU-PF that contributed to the deep crisis of the national project in the 2000s.

In the last section, the implications of the entry of MDC into national politics and the problems it confronted as it tried to install post-nationalist politics and wrestle political power from ZANU-PF are analysed. This provides the context for bringing together all the key issues and challenges facing the Zimbabwean nation-state project.

27. O.M. Tshabangu, The 11 March Movement in ZAPU-Revolution with the Revolution for Zimbabwe (York: Tiger Papers Publications, 1979), p. 2.

2. Defining the African National Project

The roots of the African national project are located in colonial encounters. The project emerged at the confluence of the complex politics of domination, resistance, mimicry, appropriation, negotiation, warfare, hybridity, and syncretism as worldviews collided and blended.[28] Diana Jeater described the colonial encounter as a phase of 'translation' – a period of constant interaction in which different elements of knowledge within different communities worked with and made sense of each other. She went on further to argue that these encounters were characterised by 'a mutual lack of recognition and understanding, expressed through both goodwill and hostility.'[29] Yash Tandon has this to say about the African national project:

> The national project, however, is not solely a nationalist strategy, but a strategy for local, national, regional and South-South self-determination, independence, dignity and solidarity. It is the essential political basis for any strategies to end aid dependence. The national project is the continuation of the struggle for independence. It is a project that began before countries in the South got their independence from colonial rule, continued for several decades after political independence, and then, in the era of globalisation, it appeared to have died a sudden death. If it has died, it needs to be revived.[30]

The African national project unfolded in phases. Prior to the Second World War, it was dominated by emerging African bourgeois elements that had undergone missionary-run education and were attracted by imperial and colonial liberal ideologies that had continued to exclude Africans on the basis of their colour. The emerging African bourgeois/elite desired inclusion in the liberal and civic benefits of the colonial system. These were being enjoyed by minority white settlers, while Africans languished as subjects rather than citizens under a decentralised despotism governed according to 'invented' but inflexible traditions and customs.[31]

The most celebrated phase of the African national project is decolonisation. The key objective was to secure liberation from foreign domination and its slogan was self-determination. Paul Tiyambe Zeleza argued that:

---

28. K.H. Chen, 'Introduction: The Decolonisation Question,' in K.H. Chen (ed.), *Trajectories: Inter-Asia Cultural Studies* (London: Routledge, 1998). See also S.J. Ndlovu-Gatsheni, 'Re-Thinking the Colonial Encounter in Zimbabwe in the Early Twentieth Century,' in *Journal of Southern African Studies*, 33 (1) (March 2007), pp. 17391.
29. D. Jeater, *Law, Language and Science: The Invention of the 'Native Mind' in Southern Rhodesia*, 1890–1930 (Portsmouth NH: Heinemann, 2007), pp. 1–3.
30. Y. Tandon, *Ending Aid Dependence* (Oxford: Fahamu Books, 2008), p. 66.
31. M. Mamdani, *Citizen and Subject: Contemporary Africa and the Legacy of Late Colonialism* (Princeton NJ: Princeton University Press, 1996).

> The wholesale repudiation of nationalism, and it proudest moment, decolonisation –whether in the name of the juggernaut of globalisation or the anti-foundationalism of the 'posts' – is ultimately a disavowal of history, an act of wilful amnesia against the past and the future. Against the past because it forgets, in the case of Africa, that the progressive nationalist project, which is far from realisation, has always had many dimensions in terms of its social and spatial referents.[32]

Zeleza went further to argue that African nationalism was never simply a representational discourse: it involved concrete struggles over material resources and moral possibilities. Despite its internal inconsistencies and contestations, the African nationalist imaginary sought to achieve decolonisation, nation-building, development, democracy and regional integration.[33] However, the trajectory of the African national project became complicated during the period when political independence was achieved. As noted by Tandon:

> After independence ... [p]eople who fought and won independence, involving huge sacrifices ... began to ask their political leaders and intellectuals some critical questions: Where do we go from here? What now? What do we do with this hard won independence? There also came to the surface even more difficult questions about self-identity that had been subdued during the struggle for independence: Who are we as a 'nation'? How do we forge nationhood out of disparate ethnic, racial, religious linguistic, regional and sub-regional groupings?[34]

Indeed, by the end of the Cold War the African national project had run aground, prompting Thandika Mkandawire to argue that:

> In recent years, both nationalism and its main projects have fallen on hard times – betrayed by some of its heroes, undercut by international institutions and the forces of globalisation, reviled and caricatured by academics, and alien to a whole new generation of Africans born after independence. In intellectual circles, nationalism stands accused of a whole range of crimes and misdeeds. And yet in defiance of its death foretold, nationalism in Africa and elsewhere has displayed a remarkably enduring resonance, although in the eyes of some incongruously and regrettably so. Some of the metamorphosis it has undergone, however, has rendered it far removed from the original version that people like Julius Nyerere represented.[35]

32. P.T. Zeleza, *Rethinking Africa's 'Globalisation': Volume 1: The Intellectual Challenges* (Trenton NJ: Africa World Press, 2003).
33. Ibid.
34. Tandon, *Ending Dependence*, p. 67.
35. T. Mkandawire, 'African Intellectuals and Nationalism,' in T. Mkandawire (ed.), *African Intellectuals: Rethinking Politics, Language, Gender and Development* (London: Zed, 2005), p. 2.

The African national project is described as a 'project' because of its being 'work-in-progress' since the end of the Second World War. Much 'unfinished business' remains. Its tasks can be summarised in the following key questions: How to forge national consciousness out of a multiplicity of racial and ethnic groups enclosed within the colonial state boundaries? How to fashion a suitable model of governance relevant to societies emerging from colonialism? What models of economic development are relevant to the promotion of rapid economic growth to extricate postcolonial states from underdevelopment? What role was the independent African postcolonial state to play in the economy and society? How might the new African political leaders promote popular democracy that was denied under colonialism? What type of relationship was to be maintained between the ex-colonies and the ex-colonial powers and other developed nations of the world without being dependent on aid?

No wonder, then, that at the centre of the African national project is the challenge of specifying who belongs to the nation together with the task of defining the criteria for citizenship. Amina Mama noted that identity is about power and resistance, subjection and citizenship, action and reaction.[36] African nationalism has tried to sort out these issues of who belongs to the nation and of defining criteria for citizenship through complex practices of rendering visible those non-conforming elements for purposes of assimilation as well as eliminating those found to be too inflexible to be accommodated within particular nationalist imaginaries. Deployment of physical violence has been part of the progression of nationalism as it subordinated some identities and histories to its agenda. Physical violence was often resorted to where other symbolic forms of violence meant to highlight and then obliterate differences had failed.[37]

African nationalism, like other nationalisms, is a quintessentially homogenising, differentiating and classifying discourse. The nature of nationalism provoked postcolonial thinkers to challenge the ways in which coercion and violence were deployed to produce people as subjects of the nation. Ideally, nationalism aims at producing homogenised people through totalisation of certain human characteristics, such as language, race and culture, into common attributes that define a national community.[38] So far, this approach has not succeeded as a response to the key tasks of the national project and the key questions outlined above.

The attempt to respond to the main questions of the national project has

36. A. Mama, 'Challenging Subjects: Gender and Power in African Context', in H. Melber (ed.), *Identity and Beyond: Rethinking Africanity* (Uppsala: Nordic Africa Institute, 2001), p. 13.
37. K. Verdery, 'Whither "Nation" and "Nationalism?"', in G. Balakrishnan and B. Anderson (eds), *Mapping the Nation* (London and New York: Verso, 1996), p. 227.
38. Ibid.

given birth to many imaginations of freedom and liberation ranging from the nativist, the liberal, the socialist, the popular democratic, the theocratic and the transnational prescriptive models.[39] Looming over these internal African prescriptive models were various versions of pan-Africanism that included the Trans-Atlantic, Black Atlantic, continental, sub-Saharan, Pan-Arab and global imaginations.[40] It is within this broader context of overlapping and intersecting antinomies within African liberation thought and the continual search for models through which sovereignty, self-determination, economic development, state-making and nation-building as well as usable democracy could be achieved that the African national project has remained unfinished business and a continual work-in-progress. As argued by Fantu Cheru, there is also the element of continual search for policy space within which Africans were/are able to take control of their destiny.[41] This is the broader terrain within which the Zimbabwean nation-state project can be understood and its problems made sense of.

39. P.T. Zeleza, 'Imagining and Inventing the Postcolonial State in Africa,' in *Contours: A Journal of African Diaspora* in http://www.press.uillionnois.edu/journal/contours/1.1/zeleza.html
40. P.T. Zeleza, 'Pan-Africanism' in P.T. Zeleza and D. Eyoh (eds), *Encyclopaedia of Twentieth Century African History* (London and New York: Routledge, 2003), pp. 415–18.
41. F. Cheru, 'Development in Africa: The Imperial Project versus the National Project and the Need for Policy Space' in *Review of African Political Economy*, 120 (2009), pp. 275–8.

3. Background: Emergence of Identities

The Zimbabwean nation-state project cannot be fully understood without a clear understanding of the identity terrain in which it emerged. This complex terrain is constituted by a combination of pre-colonial, colonial, nationalist and post-colonial historical interludes, which form the background to the emergence and politicisation of identities in Zimbabwe. The historian David Norman Beach argued that the vast region lying between the Zambezi and Limpopo Rivers from as early as the 10th to the mid-20th centuries CE witnessed the immigration of different peoples, who included the ancestors of the Shona, Nguni and other groups that have left an indelible ethnic imprint on modern Zimbabwe.[42] As a result of pre-colonial historical processes of migration and settlement, Zimbabwe developed socially into a multi-ethnic society inhabited by the Shangani/Tsonga/Hlengwe in the southeastern parts of the Zimbabwean plateau; the Venda in the south and border lands with South Africa; the Tonga in the north and borderland with Zambia; and the Kalanga, Sotho-Tswana and Ndebele in the southwest.

The numerically dominant group, collectively termed Shona, are also dispersed spatially and linguistically among the Karanga, inhabiting the southern parts of the plateau, including Masvingo province. The Zezuru and Korekore inhabit the northern and central parts of the plateau (Mashonaland West, East and Central provinces), and the Manyika and Ndau the east, covering the areas known as Manicaland and Chipinge, and stretching to the border with Mozambique.[43] On the language ecology of the country, Finex Ndhlovu has written that 'Zimbabwe is a multilingual country with eighteen African languages that include Shona, Ndebele, Kalanga, Nambya, Tonga, Sotho, Dombe, Xhosa, Tonga of Mudzi, Venda, Shangani, Tshwawo, Tswana, Barwe, Sena, Doma, Chikunda and Chewa.'[44] However, Shona and Ndebele have come to be the dominant national languages, alongside English as the official one.

What is known about identities prior to colonialism is that they were very fluid, permeated by complex processes of assimilation, incorporation, conquest of weaker groups by powerful ones, inter- and intra-marriage, alliances, fragmentation and constant movement. Identities that crystallised in this complex milieu were social and moral in character rather than solid and political. Identities founded on moral

42. D.N. Beach, *The Shona and Their Neighbours* (Oxford: Blackwell, 1994), p. 78; and D.N. Beach, *A Zimbabwean Past: Shona Dynastic Histories and Oral Traditions* (Gweru: Mambo Press, 1994).

43. D.N. Beach, *Zimbabwe Before 1900* (Gweru: Mambo Press, 1984); and T.O. Ranger, 'Missionaries, Migrants and the Manyika: The Invention of Ethnicity in Zimbabwe', in Leroy Vail (ed.), *The Creation of Tribalism in Southern Africa* (London: James Currey, 1989).

44. F. Ndhlovu, 'Gramsci, Doke and the Marginalisation of the Ndebele Language in Zimbabwe', *Journal of Multilingual and Multicultural Development,* 27 (4) (2006), 305. See also S.J. Hachipola, *A Survey of the Minority Languages of Zimbabwe* (Harare: University of Zimbabwe Publications, 1998).

imperatives had more to do with culture, communal security and social membership, as opposed to political identities mediated by competitive confrontation over material resources and political power.[45] On the fluidity and flexibility of pre-colonial identities, Ranger argued, 'before colonialism Africa was characterised by pluralism, flexibility, multiple identities; after it African identities of "tribe," gender and generation were all bounded by the rigidities of invented tradition.'[46]

Colonialism had the negative effect not of inventing identities from scratch, but reinventing existing ones, rigidifying and politicising them in a number of ways. This subject has attracted the attention of Mahmood Mamdani, who ably demonstrated empirically and conceptually how colonialism constructed 'ethnic citizenship' in Africa.[47] Mamdani noted that the advent of settler-colonialism entailed differentiation of people within the boundaries of colonies according to race. This culminated in the development of the colonial state as a bifurcated phenomenon governing citizens and subjects differently. Citizens (white settlers) were governed through urban civil power, and this enabled them to enjoy all the fruits of civil and political freedoms and liberties. The subjects (natives/black Africans) were governed through 'decentralised despotism' permeated by tradition and customary order and overseen by a rural chiefly authority as the lowest ranking and salaried colonial official. Under this decentralised structure, Africans were fragmented into rigidified ethnic groups.[48]

In the particular case of Rhodesian colonialism, the population was categorised into Europeans, Asians, coloured and native peoples. The natives were further categorised into 'aboriginal natives' and 'colonial natives,' the 'Mashona natives' and the 'Matabele natives.'[49] This was part of creating 'ethnic citizenship' that was regulated through a 'regime of ethnic rights.'[50] Ethnic citizenship was enforced through the national identity card system that coded and classified Africans according to an assigned village and district of origin. Under this system, every 'native district' in Rhodesia was represented by a specific numerical code and every adult 'native' was issued a national identity card known

45. J. Lonsdale, 'The Moral Economy of Mau Mau', in B. Berman and J. Lonsdale (eds), *Unhappy Valley: Conflict in Kenya and Africa* (London: James Currey, 1992); J. Lonsdale, 'Moral and Political Argument in Kenya', in B. Bernam, D. Eyoh, and W. Kymlika (eds), *Ethnicity and Democracy in Africa* (Oxford: James Currey, 2004), pp. 73–95.

46. T. Ranger, 'The Invention of Tradition Revisited: The Case of Colonial Africa', in Ranger and Vaughan (eds), *Legitimacy and the State* (London: Macmillan Press, 1993), p. 63.

47. M. Mamdani, *Citizen and Subject: Contemporary Africa and the Legacy of Late Colonialism* (Princeton NJ: Princeton University Press, 1996).

48. Ibid., p. 18. See also M. Mamdani, *When Victims Become Killers: Colonialism, Nativism, and the Genocide in Rwanda* (Oxford: James Currey, 2001).

49. Southern Rhodesia, *Statute of Law of Southern Rhodesia: Volume 7* (Salisbury: Government Printer, 1963).

50. S.J. Ndlovu-Gatsheni, 'How Europe Ruled Africa: Matabeleland Region of Zimbabwe', *International Journal of Humanistic Studies,* 5 (2006), pp. 1–18.

as *isithupha* in Ndebele and *chitupa* in Shona. This document provided details of one's chief, village of origin and district of ancestral origin.[51] Additionally, the colonial state went further and formulated an ethnicised wage differential system within which 'native' workers were ethnically differentiated for specific jobs. This practice was rampant in the mines, where Shangani were stereotyped as the 'best workers above and below ground,' the Ndebele were said to be the best 'foremen' and the Manyika were said to be 'best house servants.'[52]

Both historians and language specialists have shown how missionaries and the colonial drive to standardise 'native' languages contributed significantly to the invention of ethnicity.[53] Vernacular languages had to be codified and orthography established for missionary, educational and administrative purposes. In 1929, the Rhodesian government commissioned Clement M. Doke to research the language varieties spoken by 'natives' for purposes of standardisation into monolithic and homogenous linguistic categories. As Doke himself put it, his purpose was 'a settlement of the language problems involving the unification of the dialects into a literary form for educational purposes, and the standardisation of a uniform orthography for the whole area.' He went on further to brag that 'natives were placed at my disposal for investigations, and information was most readily supplied.'[54]

Doke's work in the 'invention' of standard Shona culminated in the *Report on the Unification of Shona Dialects* of 1931 that created what is today called the Shona language, and indirectly contributed to the manufacturing of a greater regional Shona identity that today stands in polar opposition to the equally manufactured greater Ndebele regional identity.[55] Solomon Mombeshora captured the overall contribution of colonialism to the identity problems in Zimbabwe by stating that 'the seeds of ethnic factor were derived from the pre-colonial past, [but] the colonial era provided fertile soil in which the ideology of tribalism germinated, blossomed and was further propagated.[56]

51. Muzondidya and Ndlovu-Gatsheni, 'Echoing Silences', p. 279.
52. Ranger, 'Missionaries, Migrants and the Manyika'; and T. Yoshikuni, *African Urban Experiences in Colonial Zimbabwe: A Social History of Harare before 1925* (Harare: Weaver Press, 2007).
53. Ranger, 'Missionaries, Migrants and the Manyika'; T. Ranger, *The Creation of Tribalism in Zimbabwe* (Gweru: Mambo Press, 1985); H. Chimhundu, 'Early Missionaries and the Ethnolinguistic Factor During the "Invention of Tribalism" in Zimbabwe', *Journal of African History,* 33 (1) (1992), pp. 103–29; and Ndhlovu, 'Gramsci, Doke and the Marginalisation of the Ndebele Language in Zimbabwe', pp. 305–18.
54. C.M. Doke, *A Comparative Study in Shona Phonetics* (Johannesburg: University of Witwatersrand Press, 1931), p. iii.
55. C.M. Doke, *Report on the Unification of the Shona Dialects* (Hartford: Stephen Austin and Sons, 1931).
56. S. Mombeshora, 'The Salience of Ethnicity in Political Development: The Case of Zimbabwe', *International Sociology,* 5 (4) (1990), p. 431.

This background is important for understanding the problems that confronted Zimbabwean nationalism in its endeavour to forge a common national identity. The imagined common national identity (Zimbabwean) could not be easily manufactured within a colonial environment in which ethnic identities were deliberately politicised. Colonialism never intended to create nations in Africa based on common national identity. Instead, colonialism wanted to create colonial states as 'neo-Europes' that served metropolitan material needs while keeping Africans in numerous fragmented 'tribes' and unable to unite against colonial oppression and domination. But besides the contribution of colonialism to the politicisation of ethnicity, the memories and histories of multiple layers of malignant and contested histories stretching from Great Zimbabwe through to the present did not make it easy to forge the monolithic Zimbabwean identity required by nationalists.

Gerald C. Mazarire has recently argued that:

> ... the pre-colonial history of Zimbabwe is best appreciated from breaking points or those contexts of build up and fragmentation already written in the larger narratives of the 'rise and fall' of states where new identities emerge and old ones are transformed, negotiated or accommodated.[57]

This prescient analysis is very relevant to a new understanding of the issue of identities in postcolonial Zimbabwe. Mazarire has embarked on a refreshing and radical historical process of exploring and debunking previous intellectual historical endeavours predicated on homogenising otherwise heterogeneous histories of the pre-colonial people found between the Zambezi and Limpopo Rivers.

Mazarire engaged with how Shona identity is a conflation of linguistic, cultural and political attributes of a people who did not even know themselves by that name until the late 19th century. What is today homogenised as Shona is an amalgam of people who were variously described as 'vaNyai,' 'abeTshabi,' 'Karanga' or 'Hole.'[58] Jocelyn Alexander described the idea of a homogenised 'Shona' identity as 'an anachronistic label applied to a diverse range of groups with no single cultural or political identity.'[59] One can add that in the southwest of the Zimbabwe plateau there emerged another hegemonic identity known as Ndebele that conflated and homogenised such identities as Kalanga, Nyubi, Venda, Tonga, Tswana, Sotho, Birwa and Lozwi into a broad Ndebele iden-

57. G.C. Mazarire, 'Pre-Colonial Zimbabwe: Some Reflections', in B. Raftopoulos and A.S. Mlambo (eds), *Becoming Zimbabwe: A History of Zimbabwe from Pre-colonial Times to 2008* (Harare: Weaver Press, 2009).
58. Ibid.
59. J. Alexander, *The Unsettled Land: State-Making and the Politics of Land in Zimbabwe, 1893–2003* (London: James Currey, 2006), p. 19.

tity. Without this deconstruction of the historical processes of enlargement and homogenisation of identities, a false view of a Zimbabwe as being divided into 'Shona' and 'Ndebele' identities will persist. Zimbabwe has already paid dearly for freezing people into this conflict and into suspicion-ridden bimodal ethnicity, as evidenced by the low intensity 'civil war' that engulfed Matabeleland and the Midlands regions in the 1980s.[60]

Nationalist discourses of nation-building favoured unitary histories on which to base the imagined postcolonial nation. In the process, they ceaselessly constructed national nodal points on which to hinge and construct national identity. Some historians deliberately sought to construct a national rather than tribal history of Zimbabwe in which the Ndebele and the Shona united against colonialism in 1896 and 1897.[61] Ray S. Roberts criticised the work of Terence Ranger for sustaining a linear unitary history running from 'Mukwati to Nkomo/Mugabe.' For him, Ranger produced a political history of Zimbabwe that fell into the old-fashioned Whiggish mould of Panglossian unilinear development.[62]

The reality, however, is that Ranger's subsequent work did not amount to the creation of nationalism, but to critical analysis of the making of nationalism. For instance, Ranger explained how Joshua Nkomo (a leading Zimbabwean nationalist) became fascinated with identities to the extent of becoming 'a leading member' of the Kalanga Cultural Promotion Society and of the Matabeleland Home Society (MHS) as well as of the Southern Rhodesia African National Congress. His identity at home was Kalanga; in Bulawayo it was Ndebele; in Rhodesia as a whole it was nationalist.'[63] Ranger celebrated Nkomo's belief in possibilities and the desirability of one person having multiple identities and 'possessing such a hierarchy of identities, each deep and valid and each enriching the other,' and concluded that 'Nkomo was a great synthesiser.'[64]

But Zimbabwean nationalism failed to continue the progressive process of 'synthesising' different identities as a logical way to arrive at a common identity.

60. Catholic Commission for Justice and Peace (CCJP) and Legal Resources Foundation (LRF), *Breaking the Silence, Building True Peace: Report on the Disturbances in Matabeleland and the Midlands, 1980–1989* (Harare: CCJP and LRF, 1997); and B. Lindgren, 'The Politics of Identity and the Remembrance of Violence: Ethnicity and Gender at the Installation of a Female Chief in Zimbabwe', in V. Broch-Due (ed.), *Violence and Belonging: The Quest for Identity in Post-Colonial Africa* (London and New York: Routledge, 2005).

61. T. Ranger, *Revolt in Southern Rhodesia: A Study in African Resistance* (London: Heinemann, 1967).

62. R.S. Roberts, 'Traditional Paramontcy and Modern Politics in Matabeleland: The End of the Lobengula Royal Family – and of Ndebele Particularism?', *Heritage of Zimbabwe*, 24 (2005), p. 30.

63. Ranger, *Voices from the Rocks*, pp. 210–11.

64. Ibid., p. 211.

Added to this, scholars like Masipula Sithole brought themselves into the bimodal ethnic categorisation of Zimbabwe to the extent that Sithole even conflated the 'Shangani' identity with the 'Shona' identity. This is revealed in his analysis of ethnic groupings within nationalist movements and his listing of Sitholes as 'Shona.'[65] The progression of Zimbabwean nationalism has fossilised along these false Ndebele-Shona ethnic fault-lines, with devastating implications for the postcolonial nation-building project.

In the 1990s, a very xenophobic document entitled 'For Restricted Circulation: Progress Review on the 1979 Grand Plan' that defined the nationalist struggle as nothing but a Shona affair to establish Shona hegemony in Zimbabwe, circulated within the country. It read in part:

> The Ndebeles had no legal claim whatsoever upon Zimbabwean sovereignty just like their earlier cousins (followers of Soshangane) later led by Ndabaningi Sithole, that hobgoblin who tried to hijack the struggle. Sithole was foiled and summarily ejected from the party – an act he regretted till his grave ... ZANU's correction of Sithole's errors left the Shangaans a thoroughly confused group despite the modification of their identity to drift closer to Shona under the guise of a language called Ndau, generally accepted among the ignorant as a dialect of Shona. The truth remains – they are foreigners, unwilling to advance our cause as they huddle around and cling childishly to the 'Ndonga.'[66]

It was not clear who the author of this document was. Its origins were roughly linked to Shona-speaking intellectuals based in the United Kingdom in the late 1970s, who were said to have imagined independent Zimbabwe as a Shona republic in which the Ndebele were to be dominated in every aspect of life, if not completely eliminated. While ZANU-PF dismissed the document as a product of imperialist plans to divide the country, it deeply infuriated those Ndebele-speaking people that had access to it. The document even celebrated the *Gukurahundi* conflict that left over 20,000 Ndebele civilians dead in the period between 1980 and 1987. It left an impression that *Gukurahundi* was part of a ZANU-PF Grand Plan to eliminate the Ndebele. But what is important about this 'mysterious' document is that it tapped into some deep historical issues about identities, linking them back to their pre-colonial origins. It expressed the way in which many Zimbabwean nationalists chose to act within the nationalist movements without uttering words and sometimes masking such manoeuvres as ideological differences.

65. M. Sithole, *Zimbabwe: Struggles within the Struggle: Second Edition* (Harare: Rujeko Publishers, 1999).
66. This document 'For Restricted Circulation: Progress Review on the 1979 Grand Plan' has no clear author. The original Grand Plan is said to have been written by 'Shona' intellectuals based in the United Kingdom towards the end of the liberation struggle as a secret ZANU-PF policy.

Apart from Sithole in his *Struggles within the Struggle* that documented the pulsations of ethnic identities among the rank and file of liberation movements, Zimbabwean historians have been reluctant to engage directly with issues of identities. This led James Muzondidya and the current author to argue that:

> Until recently, Zimbabweans have been conspicuously silent about questions of ethnicity. As in the colonial period, especially during the days of the nationalist liberation struggle, all attempts to discuss ethnic identities, especially their manifestation in the political and economic spheres, were brushed aside. Yet, ethnicity has continued to shape and influence the economic, social and political life of Zimbabwe since the achievement of independence in 1980.[67]

However, in recent years, Enocent Msindo boldly engaged in uncoupling Ndebele and Kalanga identities in the southwestern part of the country, thereby inaugurating a deconstruction of the regional 'Ndebele' identity. Introducing his study of ethnicity in Matabeleland, Msindo wrote:

> The history of Matabeleland is one of a restless frontier where identities (ethnicity, regional and/or national) shifted and got different meanings in different historical contexts. It is not simply a *Ndebele* history, but a complicated history of many ethnic groups that have never attracted the scholarly attention of researchers who simply work under the illusion that Matabeleland is *Ndebele* land.[68]

While nationalism was meant to forge a common national identity as part of the imagination of the postcolonial nation, it quickly ran up against resilient local and regional identities that needed careful negotiation or marshalling into a common national identity. It became very hard for nationalism to ignore some identities with a pre-colonial origin. In the heyday of unitary mass nationalism (1957–62), the chairman of the Cultural Club that organised the Zimbabwe Festival of African Culture held in May 1963 stated that:

> We are descended from the great civilisation of the Monomotapa Empire which even today enriches the archives of this land and literature of the Portuguese and Arab peoples. Let that be known by those who wish us ill or well. Let those who pour scorn and derision on this our modest beginning, know that we shall work untiringly to make Zimbabwe the heart of African culture.[69]

Some historians even tried to interpret the postcolonial Zimbabwe state as a successor to pre-colonial Munhumutapa, in the process conflating 'Karanga'

67. J. Muzondidya and S.J. Ndlovu-Gatsheni, 'Echoing Silences': Ethnicity in Postcolonial Zimbabwe, 1980–2007', *African Journal on Conflict Resolution: Special Issue on Identity and Cultural Diversity in Conflict Resolution in Africa,* 7 (2) (2007), p. 276.
68. E. Msindo, 'Ethnicity in Matabeleland, Zimbabwe: A Study of Kalanga–Ndebele Relations, 1860s–1980s' (unpublished PhD thesis, University of Cambridge, August 2004), p. 1.
69. Quoted in Turino, *Nationalists, Cosmopolitans and Popular Music in Zimbabwe,* p. 181.

and 'Shona,' and 'Shona' and 'authentic' Zimbabwean. Stan Mudenge wrote that postcolonial Zimbabwe was 'not merely a geographical expression created by imperialism during the nineteenth century.' To him, it was 'a reality that has existed for centuries, with a language, a culture and a "world view" of its own, representing the inner core of the Shona historical experience.'[70] The danger of popularising such a primordial origin of Zimbabwe is that it tends to obliterate or suppress other histories. For instance, how could those who did not belong to the pre-colonial Munhumutapa celebrate its revival in 1980 as Zimbabwe cloaked under the banner of territorial nationalism?

In addition to the sensitive issue of ethnicity is that of race, which is equally important to the debate on forging a national identity in the context of a colonial environment. Edward Said identified three lines along which the crystallisation of native/colonised political awareness of identity was being developed. He saw it developing from a point where the colonised 'become a willing servant of imperialism (a native informant), to the awareness and acceptance of the past without allowing it to prevent future developments and finally to striving to shed off colonial self in search for the essential and authentic pre-colonial self.'[71]

As the colonised natives vigorously searched for lost identities, nationalism developed in opposition to colonialism and the white settler. Kuan-Hsing Chen argued that the African struggle for identity is shaped by 'the immanent logic of colonialism,' making it inevitable that colonised people's nationalism reproduce 'racial and ethnic discrimination; a price to be paid by the coloniser as well as the colonised selves.'[72] With specific reference to Africa, Mahmood Mamdani explored this entanglement of race in struggles for national identity as the 'native-settler' question, adding that:

> The settler-native question is a political question. It is also a historical question. Settlers and natives belong together. You cannot have one without the other, for it is the relationship between them that makes one a settler and the other a native. To do away with one, you have to do away with the other.[73]

The settler presence in Rhodesia meant that the crystallisation of nationalism and the concomitant issue of identity was permeated by race. The daunting task for African nationalists as nation-builders in ex-settler colonies like South Africa and Zimbabwe is to create a stable, common and single citizenship for settlers and natives. This task involves more than de-racialising institutions and

70. S.I.G. Mudenge, *A Political History of Munhumutapa* (Harare: Zimbabwe Publishing House, 1988), pp. 362–4.
71. E.E. Said, *Culture and Imperialism* (London: Chatto and Windus, 1993), p. 258.
72. K.H. Chen, 'Introduction: The Decolonisation Question', in K.H. Chen (ed.), *Trajectories: Inter-Asia Cultural Studies* (London: Routledge, 1998), p. 14.
73. M. Mamdani, 'When Does a Settler Become a Native? Citizenship and Identity in a Settler Society', *Pretext: Literacy and Cultural Studies,* 10 (1) (July 2001), pp. 63–73.

removing racial legislation from the statute books. It requires what Mamdani has termed 'an overall metamorphosis' within which 'erstwhile colonisers and colonised are politically reborn as equal members of a single political community.'[74] For both Zimbabwe and South Africa, the African nationalists have attempted to use the policy of reconciliation as a methodology of bringing the former 'native' and the former 'settler' into common citizenship. This has proven to be an inadequate formula. What is lacking is the building of a new political order that is not tainted by colonial and apartheid legacies and is based on consent rather than conquest, capable of creating equal and consenting citizens.[75]

Mamdani's analysis reveals the crucial challenges inherent in the formation and construction of common national identities, and in forging common citizenship out of different races. Forging common identity and common citizenship out of different ethnic groups is equally difficult. Nationalism has proven inadequate to the task. Jocelyn Alexander, Joan McGregor and Terence Ranger in *Violence and Memory* grappled with the meaning of nationalism. Starting from the perspective that nationalism was 'a notoriously protean term,' they proffered two contextual definitions: 'A minimal definition of nationalism, of course, is support for the sequence of mass nationalist parties – over the thirty years from the ANC's relaunch in 1957 to Zapu's merger with Zanu in 1987.'[76] What was 'nationalist' about such parties as SRANC, NDP, ZAPU, and ZANU was their anti-colonial stance and espousal of an ideology of a national right to land, and their pandering to the idea of an African nation and liberation.[77]

74. Ibid.
75. Ibid.
76. J. Alexander, J. McGregor, and T. Ranger, *Violence and Memory: One Hundred Years in the 'Dark Forests' of Matabeleland* (London: James Currey, 2000), p. 84.
77. Ibid., pp. 84–5.

4. Becoming National: Race, Ethnicity and Elusive Unity

Amina Mama argued that 'identity is at best a gross simplification of self-hood, a denial and negation of the complexity and multiplicity at the roots of most African communities.'[78] She proceeded to note that 'not only is there no all-encompassing concept of identity in much of Africa, but there is no substantive apparatus for the production of the kind of singularity that the term seemed to require.'[79] Nationalism was one of the main vehicles for constructing national identities out of different ethnic and racial groups. Zimbabwe's major nationalist parties remained vague about issues of belonging and criteria for citizenship beyond the simple formula of 'one man one vote.' The use of the term 'man' captured what Mama termed 'unitary (masculine) notions of patriotism, national unity and integration' predicated on 'restorationist appeals to implicitly masculine constructions of African culture.'[80]

With specific focus on Zimbabwe, Msindo argued that the founding fathers of the nationalist parties used nationalism loosely, without clearly defining the nation, adding that:

> They were not clear who the future national citizens were to be, and to them, it does seem nationalism was a desire for freedom, justice and self-governance. The project required an imagined collective Zimbabwean community of *abantwana benhlabathi* (children of the soil/land), transcending ethnicities. Interestingly, this definition was flouted by the very people who coined it, making it difficult to assert that there was any founded collective ideology of 'the nation' as we know it intellectually.[81]

Msindo posed crucial questions about nationalism's mission in Zimbabwe prior to independence:

> Was nationalism just about anti-colonialism or simply the desire for independence? In which case did it become a struggle for power? Was it mere xenophobia, justifying an anti-white stance? ... Alternatively, was it about defining a nation in which questions such as 'Who are we?' and 'Who should be part of the nation?' became issues in those years?[82]

78. A. Mama, 'Challenging Subjects: Gender and Power in African Contexts', in H. Melber (ed.), *Identity and Beyond: Rethinking Africanity* (Uppsala: Nordic Africa Institute, 2001), p. 11.
79. Ibid., p. 10.
80. Ibid., p. 12.
81. E. Msindo, 'Ethnicity in Matabeleland, Zimbabwe: A Study of Kalanga–Ndebele Relations, 1860s-1980s' (unpublished PhD thesis, University of Cambridge, 2004), p. 21.
82. Ibid., p. 21.

To respond to these questions one needs to analyse how the nationalist parties and the nationalist actors defined and articulated the pertinent issues of nation, national identity, citizenship and democracy.

The SRANC was the first mass nationalist party to emerge in Rhodesia. Its ideological position was framed within a very moderate and conservative liberal imagination of liberation and definition of citizenship. From its existing political documents, it emerged that the issue of national belonging was not given careful thought. SRANC's statement of principles had this to say on national identities:

> Its aim is the NATIONAL UNITY of all inhabitants of the country in true partnership regardless of race, colour and creed. It stands for a completely integrated society, equality of opportunity in every sphere and the social, economic and political advancement of all. It regards these objectives as the essential foundation of that partnership between people of all races without which there can be no peaceful progress in this country.

The Congress affirmed complete loyalty to the Crown as the symbol of national unity and maintained that it was not a racial movement. Its pronouncements opposed both tribalism and racialism to the extent of welcoming as members persons of any race who were sympathetic to its aims and objectives. It also recognised the rights of all who were citizens of the country, whether African, European, Coloured or Asian, to retain and enjoy permanently the fullest citizenship. It believed that the imagined democratic society could only advance through non-racial thinking and acting, and that an integrated society provided the only alternative to tribalism and racialism.[83]

SRANC emphasised that it was opposed to tribalism as well as racism in its imagination of an integrated nation founded on 'true partnership regardless of race, colour and creed.' There was fear by early nationalists that any panic within the white settler community would make them dig in and resist African nationalism as an anti-white phenomenon. Opposition to racism informed SRANC's policy on citizenship:

> Congress believes that full citizenship must be extended to all those of any race or colour who are lawful and permanent inhabitants of the country, and have demonstrated this through their satisfactory residence and integration in the life of the community over the course of five years' residence in the country.[84]

What is clear from SRANC's statement of principles is that it was a very moderate liberal-orientated nationalist party that was mainly focused on racism as

83. Southern Rhodesia African National Congress, 'Statement of Principles, Policy and Programme, Salisbury 1957', in Nyangoni and Nyandoro (eds), *Zimbabwe Independence Movements*, (London: R. Collings, 1979, p. 3.

84. Ibid., p. 10.

the key blockage to the formation of an integrated nation. Despite its moderate agenda, SRANC met with increased colonial repression that culminated in the declaration of a state of emergency, the banning of the party and the detention and restriction of its leadership in 1959.

SRANC was succeeded by the NDP, which was formed on the 1 January 1960 and launched in the suburb of Highfields in Salisbury (Harare). NDP defined itself as 'a political party initiated and led by Africans.' Among its aims was 'the struggle for, and attainment of freedom for African people of Southern Rhodesia,' and 'establishing and granting one man one vote for all inhabitants of Southern Rhodesia.'[85] The NDP was also committed to 'working in conjunction with other freedom organisations in Africa for the establishment and maintenance of democracy in Africa and the achievement of Pan-Africanism.'[86] While SRANC was preoccupied with anti-racism, the NDP emphasised the issue of 'one man one vote' as the solution to what became known as the 'Rhodesian Problem.'[87] Unlike SRANC, which was mainly an urban political formation, the NDP made deep inroads into rural areas and its rallies were massive.

The NDP leadership was dominated by nationalists of Kalanga ethnic extraction: Joshua Nkomo (president), George Silundika (financial secretary) and Jason Ziyaphapha Moyo (secretary general). These were powerful posts on the seven-man executive committee of the NDP. Msindo noted that while it is not clear whether there was a deliberate attempt to empower the Kalanga, 'Kalanga commoners quickly gave it an ethnic interpretation,' stating that 'this election makes us Bakalanga very happy as these men were elected to lead this party which has a membership of more than 1,000,000 people, most of whom are Bakalanga.'[88]

Pulsations and reverberations of ethnicity became strongly apparent within the NDP, indicated by the debates that emerged over the name for the imagined postcolonial nation. Because of the strong regional Ndebele identity, some people in Matabeleland imagined political independence on the basis of memories of the pre-colonial Ndebele state. Thus, they opposed the name 'Zimbabwe.' To the people of Matabeleland, this name conjured up the promotion of Shona history and memory. No wonder then that both Ndebele and Kalanga nationalist activists pushed for the name 'Matopos.' For instance, Mr. Mbobo, the secretary

85. Sketchley Samkange, Secretary General of National Democratic Party, 'Statement of Appeal by Interim President Michael Mawema, Salisbury, 1960', in Nyangoni and Nyandoro (eds), *Zimbabwe Independence Movements*, p. 21.

86. Ibid.

87. E. Windrich, *The Rhodesian Problem: A Documentary Record 1923–1973* (London and Boston: Routledge and Kegan Paul, 1975), which she defined as that of white supremacy in an African country and a 'self-governing colony in a state of rebellion' against the Crown.

88. Msindo, 'Ethnicity in Matabeleland', p. 233. See also *The Bantu Mirror*, 5 November 1960.

general of the MHS, pushed the idea of 'Matopos' as the name of the country in these words:

Both historically and traditionally [Matopos] was of greater significance and spiritual importance [so that] attempts to belittle it would be resisted by all in Matabeleland. Those leaders ... were best advised to stop thinking in tribal terms and we in Matabeleland are going to resist any imposed leadership.[89]

Msindo correctly notes that such regional concerns and tensions indicated the fragility of the emerging territorial nationalism. A split within NDP occurred, partly over issues of regional identities, when a group of Karanga nationalists broke with the NDP to form the Zimbabwe National Party (ZNP), the first political party to use the name 'Zimbabwe' for the country, despite protestations from Matabeleland. Michael Mawema, a Karanga from Fort Victoria (Masvingo), where the Zimbabwe Ruins are located, is credited with coming up with the name 'Zimbabwe' for the imagined postcolonial nation. His letter of resignation from the NDP read in part:

> I decided to resign from the NDP because of treachery, dishonesty, inconsistency and betrayal of the mandate and demands of our people at the last constitutional conference. We demanded one man one vote but Nkomo agreed with the UFP [United Federal Party] and signed for a qualitative franchise of £720; we demanded a majority representation in parliament but Nkomo signed for 15 seats in a house of 65; we demanded our land but Nkomo signed a document which excluded *our Zimbabwe. ... Being a true son of Zimbabwe* I made a public condemnation of the Nkomo-Whitehead-Sandys constitution as utterly unacceptable and I was suspended for having rejected that constitution ... I was called a Tshombe because I had not accepted the constitution which the great Nkomo had signed for ... You have been told that I was paid by the government quite large sums of money as Tranos Makombe said at Highfields, *'in order to split African unity'*, and that I was power hungry etc. ... Those who still believe and continue to support the NDP leadership are committing sins against those who suffered and died for this country because by such actions you are doing them injustice when you compromise with what they did not compromise on ... Many of those who speak against me are paid by the NDP from the money paid by the ordinary man who wants this money to be used for restoring *Zimbabweland* to the African people. How on earth can a *true son of Zimbabwe* follow men who are dishonest to the African cause? ... We wanted *our Zimbabweland* back to us but they signed a constitution without the land provision. ... Those who share the loot in the NDP will continue to sell you, but honest sons and daughters will seek for truth and join us in the *Zimbabwe National Party* [my emphasis].[90]

89. *The Bantu Mirror*, 20 August 1960.

90. Michael A. Mawema, 'Why I Resigned from the NDP to Join the Zimbabwe National Party, Salisbury 1961', in Nyangoni and Nyandoro (eds), *Zimbabwe Independence Movements*, pp. 48–50.

Mawema's letter is important in that it was the first public criticism of Nkomo's leadership by a fellow nationalist. In the second place, the letter demonstrates how Mawema was adamant that the imagined independent nation was to be called 'Zimbabwe.' Thirdly, the letter was a rehearsal for the grand split of 1963. Msindo argued that Nkomo managed to contain a major split in the NDP by outmanoeuvring the Karanga clique that had formed the ZNP by quickly bringing more Shona leaders into the upper echelons of the NDP.[91] But because of the NDP's drive to politicise rural people, it was banned on 9 December 1961.

NDP was succeeded by ZAPU within six days. ZAPU had a more tumultuous political existence before it was banned on 20 September 1962. It was the first mass nationalist party to use the name 'Zimbabwe' to signify acceptance of the name of the imagined postcolonial nation. ZAPU was both a carry-over from the NDP and also a more radical political formation, which inaugurated a period of sabotage to create panic among the white settler population as part of the pressure to grant independence to Africans. ZAPU intensified the issue of one man one vote as the foundation of democratic governance in the country, and relentlessly demanded majority rule. ZAPU also suffered in the split of 1963.[92]

Basing his analysis on the aims and objectives of ZAPU, Wellington W. Nyangoni argued that ZAPU's major significance was that it was the first African political organisation to apply the concepts of imperialism and pan-Africanism to Zimbabwean liberation.[93] Its stated aims and objectives were:

A. Aims and objectives:
i. To establish the policy of one man one vote as the basis of government in this country.
ii. To maintain the spirit of democracy and love of liberty among the people of Zimbabwe.
iii. To unite the African people so that they liberate themselves from all forms of imperialism and colonialism.
iv. To fight relentlessly for the elimination of all forms of oppression.
v. To create conditions for the economic prosperity of the people under a government based on the principle of one man one vote.
vi. To foster the development of the best values in African culture and traditions, so as to establish a desirable order.

91. Msindo, 'Ethnicity in Matabeleland', p. 234. See also M.O. West, *The Rise of an African Middle Class: Colonial Zimbabwe, 1898–1965* (Bloomington: Indiana University Press, 2002), pp. 225–6.

92. E. Sibanda, *The Zimbabwe African People's Union, 1961–87: A Political History of Insurgency in Southern Rhodesia* (Trenton NJ: Africa World Press, 2005).

93. W.W. Nyangoni, *African Nationalism in Zimbabwe (Rhodesia)* (Washington DC: University Press of America, 1977), p. 50.

B. Pan-Africanism
i. ZAPU shall instil and maintain the spirit of pan-Africanism in Zimbabwe.
ii. It shall work cooperatively with any other movement in Africa or elsewhere which fosters the spirit of pan-Africanism.
C. International
i. ZAPU shall observe, respect and promote human rights contained in the Declaration of Human Rights of the United Nations Charter.
ii. It shall maintain peaceful and friendly relations with such nations as are peaceful and friendly towards the African people in Zimbabwe.
iii. It shall cooperate with any such international forces as are genuinely engaged in the struggle for the total and immediate liquidation of colonialism and imperialism.[94]

The idea of a bloody nationalist revolution as the way of achieving independence gained popularity in 1962, and this political discourse invited the wrath of the colonial forces, which intensified their arrests of nationalist leaders. But it was the split of 1963 that had a devastating impact on the efforts to create the 'Zimbabwean' national identity. With the split, nationalism fossilised in the bimodal form of ZAPU and ZANU, behind which lay the spectre of Shona and Ndebele ethnicities. Nationalism as a unifying force had miscarried and 'black-on-black violence' was let loose. On the impact of the split on the people and the nationalist struggle for self-rule, Bishop Abel Muzorewa had this to say:

> In 1963 at the time of the split a demon invaded Zimbabwe ... The demon ravaged the entire country petrol-bombing to death and maiming innocent children, men and women ... To have a different political opinion was tantamount to witchcraft and as a result some of us lost confidence in ourselves and sacrificed self-rule.[95]

ZANU was born as a separate splinter party and it soon branded itself as a new political formation that favoured 'confrontational politics,' compared to ZAPU's reformism and politics of compromise. While ZANU tried to set itself apart from the previous parties by emphasising 'confrontation,' its approach to the issue of belonging was not radical. Like ZAPU, it defined itself as 'a non-racial union of all the peoples of Zimbabwe who share a common destiny and a common fate believing in the African character of Zimbabwe and democratic rule by the majority regardless of race, colour, creed or tribe.'[96] Under what it described as 'the ZANU State' it declared that:

94. ZAPU, *Confidential Draft Constitution of the Zimbabwe African People's Union* (Lusaka: 1968).

95. Bishop Abel Muzorewa, 'African National Council: A Broadcast Appeal to Zimbabweans at Home and Abroad, Lusaka, Zambia, 19 March 1975', in Nyangoni and Nyandoro (eds), *Zimbabwe Independence Movements*, p. 298.

96. 'Zimbabwe African National Union: Policy Statement, Salisbury, 21 August 1963', in Nyangoni and Nyandoro (eds), *Zimbabwe Independence Movements*, p. 65.

a) ZANU will establish a nationalist, democratic, socialist and pan-Africanist republic within the fraternity of African states and the British Commonwealth of Nations.
b) The only form of franchise that the ZANU republic will recognise is one based on 'one man one vote'.
c) In the organisation of the ZANU state the principles of the rule of law and separation of powers shall be strictly adhered to.
d) The ZANU republic shall be a unitary and indivisible state.
e) The ZANU republic shall be based on the principle of non-racialism.[97]

ZANU's policy on citizenship simply stated that: 'All people born in Zimbabwe or who have been citizens of Zimbabwe shall be citizens of the republic. Foreigners may qualify for citizenship under conditions prescribed in accordance with the Law of the Republic.'[98] At the ZANU inaugural congress held in Gwelo (Gweru) from 12 to 13 May 1964, its founder president, Reverend Ndabaningi Sithole, asserted that: 'ZANU which was formed on the 8th of August 1963, stands for democracy, socialism, nationalism, one man one vote, freedom, Pan-Africanism, non-racism and republicanism.'[99]

The rich documents of the various nationalist parties emphasise three issues: unity among Africans, one man one vote and non-racialism. In reality, the nationalist movements remained fragmented into ZAPU/ZIPRA, ZANU/ZANLA, Front for the Liberation of Zimbabwe (FROLIZI) and United African National Council (UANC), among many other factions. This fragmentation had a very negative impact on the crystallisation and formation of a cohesive national identity to be called 'Zimbabwean.'

To avoid engaging directly with the issue of building national identity, the major nationalist political formations spoke a common language of majority rule and one man one vote as the key nationalist trope. Joshua Nkomo, one of the most senior nationalist actors, once argued that: 'Being, as I am, an ardent exponent of majority rule, as the only and natural solution to the political, social and economic problems that beset the country, let me give a picture of the majority rule that we are struggling for.'[100]

> There is talk by some people that 'majority rule' means rule by Africans only; that Africanisation will deprive Europeans of their jobs and that there will be a general lowering of standards. To us majority rule means the extension of political rights

---

97. Ibid.
98. Ibid.
99. Rev. Ndabaningi Sithole, 'Zimbabwe African National Union: Presidential Address at the ZANU Inaugural Congress, Gwelo, 12–13 May 1964', in Nyangoni and Nyandoro (eds), *Zimbabwe Independence Movements*, p. 75.
100. Joshua Nkomo, 'The Case for Majority Rule in Rhodesia: Gonakudzingwa Camp, 1964', in C. Nyangoni and G. Nyandoro (eds), *Zimbabwe Independence Movements*, p. 99.

> to all people so that they are able to elect a Government of their own choice, irrespective of race, colour or creed of the individual forming such a government. All that matters is that a Government must consist of the majority party elected by the majority of the country's voters. 'Africanisation' means the opening of all those jobs and extension of the ceiling which had been closed to Africans, without necessarily eliminating those who at present hold such jobs, unless they choose to do so on their own accord, or are proved to be disloyal to the administration.[101]

What is clear is that the issue of nationality and citizenship was constantly and always defined in terms of Africans versus whites, as though Africans were already a collectivity pursuing a single and common political goal. The African nationalists took the issue of unity for granted, even after the split of 1963 that was followed by open 'black-on-black' violence. But in the 1970s, when political parties continued to fragment along the many fault lines of Ndebele vs. Kalanga, Kalanga vs. Shona, Karanga vs. Manyika, and Karanga vs. Zezuru, the rhetoric of unity entered the political discourses of the nationalist parties, particularly from such newcomers as Bishop Abel Muzorewa and new political formations as the Front for the Liberation of Zimbabwe (FROLIZI). Even those like ZANU that had broken away from ZAPU maintained they also stood for national unity. For instance, on 19 April 1971, the ZANU Supreme Council (*Dare*) issued a statement to the effect that: 'Our president says he supports the formation of a new party. This has been his consistent stand since 1964. He has not veered from it. He feels the formation of a new party to forge national unity is a must for Zimbabwe.'[102]

Upon the formation of FROLIZI, Nathan Shamuyarira emphasised its commitment 'to the unity of all Africans within and across borders.' He added that there were three main reasons FROLIZI was formed and the first he described as 'the imperative of national unity':

> The first reason is 'the imperative for national unity among all Zimbabweans', and to bring to an end the 'shameful chapter in the history of our struggle, in which ZAPU and ZANU were more often at each other's throats than they cared to fight the real enemy' ... The clear duty of national leadership is to forge unity by all possible means. With few exceptions, the national leadership of both ZAPU and ZANU did not accept this imperative. Instead, some of them started building tribal blocs and alliances within the peoples' nationalist movement for the sole purpose of maintaining their positions of leadership at the expense of the national revolution and national interest. In ZANU, this started in 1967 and in ZAPU in 1969. Indeed, what proved to be the main stumbling block to unity

101. Ibid., p. 104.
102. Zimbabwe African National Union Press Statement Issued by Supreme Council (Dare) on Behalf of Rev. N. Sithole, ZANU President, Lusaka, 19 April 1971,' in Nyangoni and Nyandoro (eds), *Zimbabwe Independence Movements*, p. 170.

> talks throughout 1970 was the regionalism prevalent in ZANU, and tribalism in ZAPU.[103]

However, those closer to struggle politics saw FROLIZI as nothing but a tribal political formation. They blamed Nathan Shamuyarira for championing a tribal Zezuru clique.[104] Even though some of FROLIZI's detractors derided it as the 'Front for the Liaison of Zezuru Intellectuals,' its draft constitution emphasised 'the imperative of national unity among all Zimbabweans.' FROLIZI was also very critical of ZAPU and ZANU for fragmenting the oppressed and fighting forces of liberation. Its draft constitution stated:

> The need for a progressive revolutionary movement, uniting not only ZAPU and ZANU but the masses of the people and all the revolutionary forces of Zimbabwe behind a single banner ... The formation today of FROLIZI puts an end to this sordid and self-destructive state of affairs. The struggle will from now on be waged against the enemy and oppressor, not against the Zimbabwe people.[105]

While new and smaller political formations like FROLIZI emphasised unity, ZAPU and ZANU fought over 'authenticity' and which party was more committed to the liberation of the country. Another new political formation, the African National Council (ANC), launched on 10 March 1972, also emphasised the centrality of unity and spelt out its core beliefs. The ANC was founded in the context of resistance to the Pearce Commission at a time when ZAPU and ZANU were proscribed political formations. So to ZAPU and ZANU leaders, the majority of whom were in detention, the ANC was a stop-gap measure to continue nationalist politics and fill the political vacuum created by Ian Smith's post-UDI politics of intensified repression. The ANC was also formed in a context in which disunity between ZAPU and ZANU had led to terrible violence in the towns of Salisbury (Harare) and Bulawayo. Thus, maintaining national unity became prominent in its agenda to avoid the problems created by ZAPU and ZANU. This became clear in its messages:

> This council believes in the power of the unity of the African masses in the imperative need for the opposition of those elements of forces which seek to sow the seeds of division among our people. Divided we will remain slaves and strangers in the land of our birth.[106]

103. Nathan Shamuyarira, 'Explanation of Why FROLIZI was formed', in Nyangoni and Nyandoro (eds), *Zimbabwe Independence Movements*, pp. 171–2
104. N. Bhebe, *Simon Vengayi Muzenda: The Struggle for and Liberation of Zimbabwe* (Gweru: Mambo Press, 2004).
105. 'FROLIZI Draft Constitution', in Nyangoni and Nyandoro (eds), *Zimbabwe Independence Movements*, p. 180.
106. Bishop Abel T. Muzorewa, 'African National Council: Aims and Objectives, Salisbury, 10 March 1972', in Nyangoni and Nyandoro (eds), *Zimbabwe Independence Movements*, p. 231.

Towards the end of his address at the launch of ANC, Bishop Abel Muzorewa stated:

> We challenge our African people to realise that, while we have chosen a peaceful and loving method of approach, in UNITY we have more than a bomb can achieve. Therefore, be UNITED; be UNITED until UNITY is strength and strength becomes POWER.[107]

Indeed, efforts to forge unity among major nationalist political formations remained elusive up until 1987, when PF-ZAPU was finally swallowed up by ZANU-PF. From the time of the Zimbabwe Declaration of Unity on 7 December 1974 and the formation in 1976 of the Zimbabwe People's Army (ZIPA) as the military and political outfit of the Patriotic Front (PF), unity eluded the nationalist leaders, with serious consequences for the unity of the rank and file in the nationalist movements. The demon that led to the split of 1963 was relentless and pervasive.

The untimely death of Herbert Chitepo in 1975 brought the debate on unity to the fore in the nationalist movement. Muzorewa was of the opinion that disunity had cost Chitepo his life and he called for the unity of all forces and all people under the ANC banner, declaring, 'think unity, act unity.'[108] Ndabaningi Sithole also thought Chitepo was a victim of tribalism within ZANU. He responded to the assassination by offering an analysis of tribalisation and regionalisation in ZANU since its formation in 1963, concluding that:

> When we formed ZANU in 1963, it was called the Zimbabwe African National Union, but by 1974 and at the beginning of 1975, it had become in practice 'Zimbabwe African Tribal Union' masquerading under the respectable garbs of the ZANU of 1963. The tribalised or regional Dare had therefore ceased to represent ZANU as we know it. It has come to represent in effect ZATU (Zimbabwe African Tribal Union) or ZARU (Zimbabwe African Regional Union).[109]

Sithole blamed ZANU's *Dare reChimurenga* (War Council) for the assassination of Chitepo on tribal grounds, as part of their efforts to eliminate easterners (Manyika) from influential positions. He added that:

> The problem which we now face as the new nation is essentially a tribal or regional one. The advocates of tribalised or regionalised political and military leadership can help us in this matter by joining us in the effort to detribalise or deregionalise the attitudes and outlooks of those who have been tragically misled to believe that one tribe or one region can ever be the centre of the politics of Zimbabwe. No

107. Ibid., p. 234.

108. Ibid., p. 302.

109. Rev. Ndabaningi Sithole, 'On the Assassination of Herbert Chitepo and ZANU, 10 May 1976', in Nyangoni and Nyandoro (eds), *Zimbabwe Independence Movements*, p. 310.

> tribe or region can be the centre of Zimbabwe. In other words, our basic problem is how to untribalise or unregionalise Zimbabweans whose present efforts are grossly misdirected and are a discredit to the whole national effort.[110]

When nationalism underwent re-tribalisation on the scale described by Sithole, it was difficult for different ethnic groups to coalesce into a national identity. Nationalism and the liberation war, while rhetorically pandering to the idea of a unitary nation, in reality served to politicise identities and nurture regionalism and tribalism.

The armed liberation war was fought by 'tribalised' armed men of ZIPRA, who not only dominated in Matabeleland and the Midlands regions but also tended to be largely Ndebele-Kalanga-speaking freedom fighters, and ZANLA, which dominated Mashonaland regions and was constituted of Shona-speaking cadres. While the ZIPRA operational zones were divided into the Southern and Northern Fronts, ZANLA operational zones were named after Shona pre-colonial heroes such as Nehanda, Kaguvi and Chaminuka, giving the whole struggle for national liberation a Shona-based articulation. While ZAPU/ZIPRA retained a large number of Shona cadres within its rank and file as well as in its top leadership, ZANU/ZANLA was largely dominated by Shona speakers among its rank and file and top leadership. No wonder that to ZANU/ZANLA there was no doubt that an independent Zimbabwe would be founded on Shona histories, memories and symbols.

Ngwabi Bhebe has explained why ZAPU/ZIPRA and ZANU/ZANLA nationalists and their supporters not only ended up exchanging fire at the front but also massacred each other in Tanzania and other places:

> The reason was very simple. These young men and women were trained to hate each other by their leaders, who wanted to justify the separate existence of their parties. Each party had its own Commissariat Department, whose task was to teach recruits the history of the party, how the party was different from the other, who the leaders were and how they were different from the less revolutionary or sell-out leaders of the rival party. Thus, the cadres were brought up to hate.[111]

The armed liberation struggle cast a shadow from under which militarists if not warlords emerged, as well as prophets of violence, who were not only committed to liberating the country but who ended up internalising the culture of violence and impunity, to the detriment of the development of democracy and a human rights culture. Under the shadow of exile and the armed struggle the ghost of tribalism wreaked havoc within the nationalist movements, stealthily eating the sons and daughters of the revolution and causing unnecessary division. Rever-

110. Ibid., p. 312.
111. Bhebe, *Simon Vengayi Muzenda*, p. 256.

end Ndabaningi Sithole squarely blamed tribalism as the wolf that was eating the children of the nationalist revolution. Focusing on internal conflicts within ZANU, Sithole explained how tribalisation and regionalisation diluted the nationalist perspective by turning ZANU into a 'tribally' based political formation and by unravelling Shona identity into antagonistic Karanga, Manyika, Korekore and Zezuru factions. In a damning letter, Sithole argued that:

> If the death of Herbert Chitepo is to be associated with any 'ism', it cannot be directly or immediately associated with colonialism or capitalism, but with tribalism or regionalism ... If it is to be associated with race, it can only be the African race ... I want everyone to know that this tribalism did not originate from the people at home but from the people outside Zimbabwe. The Karanga, Zezuru, Korekore, Ndau, Ndebele, Kalanga and other tribes in Zimbabwe are solidly united and determined to become a nation.[112]

The split between ZAPU and ZANU in 1963 inaugurated complicated ethnicised politics that made unity very hard to achieve among leading nationalist actors. It also laid the basis for imaginations of the nation that were bifurcated into irreconcilable 'Ndebele' and 'Shona' identities. Writing about the impact of the split, Nkomo had this to say:

> Repression created a new solidarity within the country: at home our people had never been more united. But tragically it was at this moment that divisions began to appear within our movement's organisation abroad. The problem of disunity has persisted up until today. [113]

The Organisation of African Unity (OAU) through its Liberation Committee and the leaders of the Frontline States tried hard to emphasise the issue of unity among the nationalist actors. The first initiative culminated in the signing of a unity agreement by leading nationalists in Lusaka in 1975, with Bishop Abel Muzorewa at the helm of the African National Council (ANC). Fighting forces also took initiatives to unite in the form of ZIPA. The third initiative was again pushed by leaders of the Frontline States and culminated in the Patriotic Front of 1976.

All these initiatives failed to re-establish a semblance of the unity the nationalist movement enjoyed in the period 1957–62. Instead, nationalists consistently had personality clashes and quarrelled over the question of leadership. At the end of the day, they fragmented into those who masqueraded as radicals, revo-

---

112. Rev. Ndabaningi Sithole's letter, quoted in Ranger, 'Missionaries, Migrants and the Manyika', pp. 118–19. See Louise White, *The Assassination of Herbert Chitepo: Text and Politics in Zimbabwe* (Bloomington and Indianapolis: Indiana University Press, 2003), for the debate on who assassinated Chitepo.

113. J. Nkomo, *Nkomo: The Story of My Life* (London: Methuen, 1984), p. 109

lutionaries and patriots, versus those who were dismissed as puppets, reactionaries, 'Tshombes' and sell-outs.[114]

The high point in this history of nationalist bifurcation and fragmentation was the Internal Settlement of 3 March 1978, which saw nationalists like Sithole and Muzorewa closing ranks and negotiating with Ian Smith for what they termed a less painful decolonisation.[115] The details of the Internal Settlement are given in the next section, where it is read as one way of imagining decolonisation and independence.

Zimbabwean nationalism was therefore highly contested from within and from without. Ethnicity further complicated the process, together with consistent attempts by some nationalists to discredit the nationalist visions of others as reactionary politics or outright 'selling-out' of the nationalist revolution.

114. S.J. Ndlovu-Gatsheni, 'Puppets or Patriots: A Study of Nationalist Rivalry Over the Spoils of Dying Settler Colonialism in Zimbabwe, 1977–1980', in W.J. Burszta, T. Kamusella, and S. Wojciechowski (eds), *Nationalisms Across the Globe: An Overview of Nationalism in State-Endowed and Stateless Nations: Volume II: The World* (Poznan: School of Humanities and Journalism, 2006), pp. 345–97; and S.J. Ndlovu-Gatsheni, 'Patriots, Puppets, Dissidents and the Politics of Inclusion and Exclusion in Contemporary Zimbabwe', *Eastern Africa Social Science Research Review*, XXIV (1) (January 2008), 81–108.

115. D. Chanaiwa, 'Zimbabwe: Internal Settlement in Historical Perspective', in *Decolonisation of Africa: Southern Africa and the Horn of Africa* (New York: UNESCO, 1981).

5. Forgotten Nationalists

Such nationalist political actors as Sithole and Muzorewa have continued to languish outside mainstream nationalist history. The popular view was that they represented reactionary politics and were bent on compromising the ideals of the national liberation struggle. In recovering the nationalist narratives of such ignored actors as Sithole and Muzorewa autobiographies are drawn upon as well as other of their writings that reveal their visions in the drama of the liberation of Zimbabwe. The autobiographies also capture how these nationalist actors envisioned the teleology of liberation. The same is true of memoirs as a lens for peering into the nationalist actors' 'very unusual circumstances of growing up.'[116]

Reverend Ndabaningi Sithole was not only a nationalist actor; he was also a 'historian' and theoretician of nationalism. His influential books included the widely quoted *African Nationalism* and *Roots of Revolution*. These books reveal a lot about his conception of the nationalist liberation struggle and his imagination of the nation. Sithole also wrote in defence of the widely condemned Internal Settlement in such booklets as *In Defence of the Rhodesia Constitutional Agreement: A Power Promise*.[117] He was a serious contender for the leadership of Zimbabwe until 1980. The same is true of Muzorewa, who did, in fact, become the first black prime minister of Zimbabwe-Rhodesia.

Sithole, who was not only the founder president of ZANU but who experienced detention and was also the founder commander-in-chief of ZANLA up to the mid-1970s, cannot be ignored in any new reflections on nationalism. The same is true of his counterpart in the signing of the Internal Settlement, Muzorewa, who was the overall president of the unitary nationalist outfit, the African National Council, formed in 1975. Muzorewa wrote *Rise Up and Walk: An Autobiography* in which he describes his contribution to nationalism and explains why he negotiated with Ian Smith.[118] Representations of the national liberation struggle in general have now reached a crucial stage, and other leading

116. P. Kaarsholm, 'Memoirs of a Dutiful Revolutionary: Fay Chung and the Legacies of the Zimbabwe Liberation War: An Introduction', in F. Chung, *Reliving the Second Chimurenga: Memories from the Liberation Struggle in Zimbabwe* (Uppsala: Nordic Africa Institute, 2006), p. 8.

117. N. Sithole, *African Nationalism* (London: Oxford University Press, 1959); N. Sithole, *Roots of Revolution: Scenes from Zimbabwe* (Oxford: Oxford University Press, 1970); and N. Sithole, *In Defence of the Rhodesian Constitutional Agreement: A Power Promise* (Salisbury: Graham Publishing, 1978).

118. A.T. Muzorewa, *Rise up and Walk: An Autobiography* (London: Evans Brothers Limited, 1978).

nationalist actors have also recorded their contribution to the nationalist struggle in memoirs and autobiographies.[119]

Autobiographies reveal that nationalism and the liberation struggle were sites of contestation, and show what each actor thought was his/her contribution to the struggle. However, Ibbo Mandaza warns us about the inherent characteristics and limits of autobiographical articulations and reflections on the national liberation struggle. In an introduction to Tekere's autobiography, he argued that:

> An autobiography is, by definition, a personal account, sometimes even a convenient and expedient interpretation of one's experiences and interactions. More so a political autobiography, placing as it does the political self at the centre of a given historical period or process. Biographies, too, are subject to similar qualifications, even if they are, for the most part, less valuable than autobiographies, in terms of personal insights and biases.[120]

Autobiographies take us back to the recollections of the nationalist liberation struggle as the person at the centre of events reflects on and articulates his/her relationship with others – foes and friends. All the existing political autobiographies were written from a defensive if not heroic position, in which the central actor justified almost all his/her political decisions and activities as the wisest at the time. In spite of this limitation, they provide valuable insights into such issues as conceptions of nationalism and visions of liberation.

The first example of a nationalist excluded from nationalist history in particular and political history of Zimbabwe in general is Reverend Sithole. He can be aptly described as a politician who rose to prominence and then fizzled out, rather like the poor Shakespearean player who briefly appears onstage and then is heard from no more. He changed from a radical to a moderate nationalist in the 1970s. But this does not justify his exclusion from studies of nationalism and analyses of various nationalist visions of the nation, liberation, citizenship and democracy. It is important to track his contributions to the liberation of Zimbabwe and his vision for the country.

Sithole's book *African Nationalism* is a treatise on African nationalism in general and Zimbabwean nationalism in particular. It reveals his understanding of the essence of African nationalism and its objectives. In a foreword to Sithole's book, Sir Garfield Todd, one-time prime minister of Rhodesia, had this to say: 'There will be criticisms from all sides, but anyone who really wishes to know

119. Nkomo, *Nkomo: The Story of My Life;* E. Tekere, *Edgar 2–Boy Tekere: A Life in Struggle* (Harare: SAPES Books 2005); Bhebe, *Simon Vengayi Muzenda; Chung, Re-living the Second Chimurenga;* and M. Nyagumbo, *With the People: An Autobiography from the Zimbabwe Struggle* (London: Allison and Busby, 1980).

120. Ibbo Mandaza, 'Introduction: Edgar Tekere and Zimbabwe's Struggle for Independence', in Tekere, *Edgar 2–Boy Tekere* , pp. 1–5.

what a moderate, capable, and thoughtful African thinks of the racial situation in southern Africa should read the book.'[121] Sithole's audience was the white minority population and the Western white world that was opposed to majority rule on the grounds that African nationalism was an anti-white movement. This is how he put it:

> Unfortunately the outside world, that is the Western world, do not seem to see this African nationalism in its right perspective. They think it is an anti-white movement, and therefore they are not sympathetic to it. Many African nationalists have been branded as rebels and subjected to the severest penalties for their nationalist activities.[122]

On the aspirations of Africans and the purpose of African nationalism, Sithole wrote that:

> African nationalism is directed against European domination, and not against the white man, just as Canada, Australia, New Zealand, and South Africa wanted their full independence from Britain, but without repudiating friendship with Britain ... What the African wants is not to drive away the white man, but to have his full independence. It is unfortunate that the African's move against European domination is interpreted as his hatred of the white man. ... The African hates European domination but does not hate the white man. He welcomes him. The physical presence of the white man in Africa is welcome, but his domination is unwelcome.[123]

To Sithole, African nationalism was a struggle against white supremacy that would continue until common sense prevailed – 'namely, that people, regardless of their colour or race, do not like to be treated as unwanted strangers in the land of their birth. The victory of African nationalism will therefore be the triumph of human personality and dignity.'[124]

Sithole was never a communist, and he saw nationalism as a vehicle through which Africans could become fully part of Western civilisation and Western modernity. To Sithole, Africans experienced a thirst for recognition as fellows and equals of the people of the world, and were fighting for reassertion of their human dignity, which was denied by colonialism.[125] Sithole was also hopeful that African nationalism was the logical consequence of the death of tribalism: 'African tribalism was on the way out as a result of the onslaught of industrial-

121. Sir Garfield Todd, 'Foreword', in Sithole, *African Nationalism.*
122. Sithole, *African Nationalism*, p. 23.
123. Ibid., p. 24.
124. Ibid., p. 38.
125. Ibid., p. 136.

ism, and the writing on the wall read: From tribalism – what's next? Of course, African nationalism.'[126]

Reading Sithole's *African Nationalism*, one can easily describe him as a voice of moderation who believed in multiracial partnership founded on the removal of white supremacy. Sithole was part of the early African educated elite who received not only missionary education, but also fully embraced Christianity, to the extent of being ordained as a minister. He espoused nationalism from the perspective of what Peter Ekeh has correctly described as the African bourgeois ideology of legitimation. Ekeh saw colonialism as a terrain of hegemonic contestation in which the colonising elite and colonised elite traded ideologies or interest-begotten justificatory theories of legitimation and the struggle for supremacy.[127] This is how Ekeh puts it:

> In many ways, the drama of colonisation is the history of the clash between the European colonisers and [the African] bourgeois class. Although native to Africa, the African bourgeois class depends on colonialism for its legitimacy. It accepts the principles implicit in colonialism but it rejects the foreign personnel that rule Africa. It claims to be competent enough to rule, but it has no traditional legitimacy. In order to replace the colonisers and rule its own people, it has invented a number of interest-begotten theories to justify that rule.[128]

Sithole was one of those very able inventors of 'interest-begotten' theories on behalf of nationalism. In *African Nationalism,* he began with an 'autobiographical introduction' of himself, which in simple terms tracked his search for Western education and the Christian-God.[129] This was an important aspect of African bourgeois legitimation ideologies, which included the central claim that the 'African bourgeoisie had attained sufficiently high – equal though not necessarily better – standards to take over from the Europeans, which set the pattern for mimicking Western standards.'[130] His position as a member of the early educated African elite determined his vision of liberation. This is how he enumerated 'the basic ingredients' of African nationalism:

> On examination, the basic ingredients that go to make up the present African nationalism may be enumerated as the African's desire to participate fully in the central government of the country; his desire for economic justice that recognises fully the principle of 'equal pay for equal work' regardless of the colour of the

126. N. Sithole, *African Nationalism: Second Edition* (London: Oxford University Press, 1968), p. 98.
127. E.E. Osaghae, 'Colonialism and Civil Society in Africa: The Perspective of Ekeh's Two Publics', *Voluntas*, 17 (2006), 235.
128. P.P. Ekeh, 'Colonialism and the Two Publics in Africa: A Theoretical Statement', *Comparative Studies in Society and History*, 17 (1) (1975), 96.
129. Sithole, *African Nationalism*, pp. 1–17.
130. Osaghae, 'Colonialism and Civil Society in Africa', p. 236.

> skin; his desire to have full political rights in his own country; his dislike of being treated as a stranger in the land of his birth; his dislike of being treated as a means for the white man's end; and his dislike for the laws of the country that prescribe for him a permanent position of inferiority as a human being. It is this exclusive policy of white supremacy that has created a deep dissatisfaction among the African peoples. It is this exclusive policy that has brought to the fore the African consciousness of a kind. It seems reasonable to say that the present African nationalism is, paradoxically, the child of white supremacy, the product of an exclusive policy.[131]

Sithole situated African nationalism within universal struggles for humanity, stating that 'the elevation of African status is ultimately the elevation of human status. Those who champion the African cause champion that of humanity.'[132] Some of Sithole's arguments were very controversial ones for a nationalist to espouse. For instance, his idea that:

> … while the Christian Church and the school are exploding colonialism, colonialism, by its aggressive economic programme, is busy exploding tribalism, and in collaboration with the Church and school, the job could not be done any better, nor any faster.[133]

To Sithole, 'colonialism has given birth to a new brand of African – a non-tribal African – in short, a national African.'[134] One wonders, if colonialism 'annihilated many tribal, linguistic barriers and divisions'; if it was responsible for 'the unification of African tribes'; and if it 'has brought Africa into international light,' then why was Sithole fighting against such a universalising and globalising phenomenon?[135] Such ideas confirm Ekeh's argument that early educated Africans like Sithole were not opposed to colonialism per se but to the fact that it was manned by an alien white bourgeoisie.

Sithole's active political career began when he joined such political parties as ZAPU, in which he held the position of treasurer. Like many other nationalists, he came from the teaching profession and from the Christian ministry. Sithole moved into the limelight of nationalist politics when he led a dissident intellectual group that split from ZAPU in 1963. He became the president of ZANU and soon espoused what he termed 'confrontational politics.' In justifying the split, Sithole argued that the nationalist struggle had to move away from petty and ineffective strikes into the phase of armed struggle. Sithole coined a number of slogans that helped build momentum for the transition to the armed phase

131. Sithole, *African Nationalism*, p. 37.
132. Ibid., p. 49.
133. Ibid., p. 69.
134. Ibid., p. 71.
135. Ibid., p. 74.

of the nationalist struggle. These included 'we are our own liberators and our own saviours,' which made him a sworn enemy of Ian Smith's government.[136] He enunciated the doctrine of the armed struggle, arguing that people involved in a liberation war should not fight with the idea of going home for Christmas, but should rather wage a full-time 'total war.'[137] Sithole succeeded to some extent in setting ZANU apart from ZAPU by articulating nationalist politics in very radical terms, and openly espousing confrontational politics. By the beginning of the 1970s, ZANU was challenging ZAPU in terms of its commitment to the armed liberation struggle and of getting armed men to the front.[138]

As part of the preparations for the Unilateral Declaration of Independence of 1965, Ian Smith's government decided to imprison and detain every leading nationalist political actor within the country, irrespective of whether they belonged to ZAPU or ZANU. Sithole was one of those imprisoned in 1964. Fay Chung, in her memoirs about Zimbabwe's liberation struggle, noted that 'the then president of ZANU, Ndabaningi Sithole, considered very dangerous because of his fiery rhetoric and his charisma, was kept in solitary confinement throughout the period. His only visitor was his interrogator.'[139]

But while they were in prison, the detained ZANU nationalists initiated a 'palace coup' to replace Sithole as ZANU leader. Chung traced the downfall of Sithole to his 11 years of imprisonment in which he was isolated from his colleagues. He was at the mercy of *agents provocateurs* who masqueraded as sympathetic to the nationalist cause.[140] Sithole faithfully used these agents to smuggle letters to his supporters, including one that instructed his supporters to assassinate the Rhodesian leader, Ian Smith. It was during his trial for the crime of attempted assassination, which carried a death sentence, that Sithole under cross-examination publicly renounced the use of confrontational politics and the armed struggle as a way of gaining majority rule. He repudiated the armed struggle in order to escape conviction and possible execution.[141] Sithole's denunciation of the armed liberation struggle was enthusiastically seized upon

136. Rev. N. Sithole, 'Presidential Address to the Inaugural Congress of Zimbabwe African National Union, Gwelo, 12–13 May 1964', in Nyangoni and Nyandoro (eds), *Zimbabwe Independence Movements*, pp. 75–85.
137. M.M. Mufuka, 'Rhodesia's Internal Settlement: A Tragedy', *African Affairs*, 78 (1979), 439–40.
138. *Zimbabwe Times: A Journal of the Zimbabwe African National Union* (September 1976), 1–6.
139. Chung, *Re-living the Second Chimurenga*, p. 62.
140. One was John Brumer, a Rhodesian secret service agent, and a certain woman from South Africa who visited Sithole. Sithole used them to smuggle sensitive letters from his prison cell. See Chung, *Re-living the Second Chimurenga*, pp. 105–18, where she discusses the downfall of Sithole.
141. J. Brumer, *For the President's Eyes Only* (Johannesburg: Hugh Keartland Publishers, 1971).

by his ZANU colleagues in prison to plot his replacement as ZANU leader and ZANLA commander-in-chief. Those active in plotting against him included Robert Mugabe, Edgar Tekere, Maurice Nyagumbo and others in detention.

Fay Chung, an open supporter of Robert Mugabe against Sithole as leader of ZANU, provides details of Sithole's paranoia, and his failure to cater for his fighting men and the dependants of his detained colleagues following the assassination of Chitepo. According to Chung, Sithole had lost touch with the realities of the struggle during his 11 year imprisonment. Chung further accused Sithole of being a tribalist and of taking controversial decisions, including forming his own high command known as the Zimbabwe Liberation Committee (ZLC).[142] The climax of Sithole's downfall was the *Magagao Declaration by Zimbabwe Freedom Fighters*, published in 1975, which unequivocally rejected Sithole as the leader of ZANU and ZANLA. The *Declaration* enumerated several reasons for the rejection of Sithole, including misuse of party finances, his failure to show sympathy for his followers who died at Mboroma and his unilateral action in forming a new leadership of ZANU without consulting the detained ZANU leaders.[143]

What has not emerged clearly is the role of tribalism/ethnicity in the removal of Sithole from ZANU's leadership. In ethnic terms, the Sitholes traced their descent from the Gaza, a minority group that occupied the eastern part of Zimbabwe. If Chitepo's death was the result of a planned initiative to remove the easterners (Manyika) from ZANU leadership, then Sithole's chances of surviving in such re-tribalised politics were even slimmer. This line of thought needs to be pursued in the context of Sithole's obsession with ethnic balancing within the ZANU and ZANLA leadership. As noted in the previous section, Sithole emerged from prison in 1975 and embarked on exorcising the ghost of tribalism as if he knew he was likely to be its next victim. After Chitepo's death and Sithole's dismissal, the focus of factionalism within ZANU shifted from Karanga-Manyika tensions to Zezuru-Karanga tensions.[144] Robert Mugabe, a Zezuru, was now at the helm of both ZANU and ZANLA.

Having been rejected by ZANU and ZANLA, Sithole travelled extensively abroad before coming back to Rhodesia as a very moderate nationalist, but still claiming to be the legitimate leader of ZANU and commander-in-chief of ZANLA. He refused to recognise Mugabe as the new leader of either through-

142. Chung, *Re-living the Second Chimurenga*, pp. 105–18.

143. The ZANU and ZANLA leaders based in Zambia were detained by Zambian authorities following the assassination of Chitepo in 1975. Sithole supported Kenneth Kaunda in attributing Chitepo's death to the dirty work of some ZANU members acting out of tribal impulses.

144. Bhebe, *Simon Vengayi Muzenda*, in which he traces in detail the internal struggles in ZANU.

out the liberation struggle. When he finally returned to Rhodesia in 1977, he was a bitter man, but did not give up nationalist politics. He formed a new organisation known as the African National Council (ANC-Sithole) and at times as ZANU-Sithole.

Sithole seemed to have raised considerable financial resources, as demonstrated by his ability to dispense cars and other rewards to his followers.[145] His new internal politics emphasised imagining Zimbabwe as a multiracial democracy with a mixed economy, and he linked up with Muzorewa to push for an internal settlement. However, Sithole failed to recoup his political fortunes in the 1970s as Muzorewa overshadowed him in terms of grassroots support. His political fortunes continued to decline, to the extent that he ended up as leader of a very insignificant party known as ZANU-Ndonga, ethnically supported by the Ndau in Chipinge. ZANU-PF did not accommodate Sithole, even in death. He was buried just like an ordinary man on his small farm at Mount Selinda.

Our second example is Bishop Abel Muzorewa. Muzorewa emerged from the pulpit into nationalist politics in 1972, when he was asked by the detained leaders of ZAPU and ZANU to lead African opposition to the Pearce Commission that was linked to the Smith-Home Constitutional Proposals. Africans had not been involved in the negotiation of these proposals, which excluded majority rule based on one man one vote as the foundation of governance in the country.[146] Muzorewa was chosen by both ZAPU and ZANU for this task because he was regarded as neutral, having not been involved in the politics of the split of 1963, and because he was considered to be able to unite Africans across the ZAPU and ZANU divide. Indeed, he managed to organise the people and to mount an aggressive publicity campaign against the Smith-Home Proposals.

In addition to mobilising Africans against the Smith-Home deal, the ANC was initially formed to demonstrate the power of African unity for purposes of liberation.[147] Having opposed the Pearce Commission, the ANC developed into a progressive political formation, with Muzorewa as its president. Its mission was shot through with Christian ideas, such as 'to continue our arduous journey to Zimbabwe in a Christian and non-violent manner.' The ANC presented itself as 'no more than [the] heirs to the people's struggle which has ceaselessly been waged since the imposition of alien rule in 1890.'[148]

The ANC was committed to many things, including a government that promoted the 'sanctity and practice of essential human freedom of conscience,

145. Ndlovu-Gatsheni, 'Puppets or Patriots', p. 353.
146. Ibid, p. 354.
147. A. Chambati, 'National Unity-ANC' in C.S. Banana (ed.), *Zimbabwe, 1890–1990: Turmoil and Tenacity* (Harare: College Press, 1989), pp. 147–59.
148. 'African National Council: Aims and Objectives, Salisbury, 10 March 1972', in Nyangoni and Nyandoro (eds), *Zimbabwe Independence Movements*, p. 231.

of expression, association, religion, assembly and movement of all people irrespective of colour, race or creed.' It also stood for 'non-racialism, the universal brotherhood of man under the fatherhood of God'; believed in a 'non-violent, peaceful, orderly but permanent and continuing struggle to be waged within the law and for the establishment of a constitutional government.' On democracy, the ANC believed in 'the government of the people, by the people and for the people' and 'that the rights and property of the minority should be protected' without 'the minority's amassing of social, political and economic privileges at the expense of the freedom of the majority.'[149] In line with these objectives and aims, Muzorewa began the search for a peaceful resolution of the Rhodesia problem, which necessarily involved negotiations with Ian Smith.

But the ANC, just like ZAPU and ZANU, was not immune to factionalism and fragmentation, especially because it contained ZAPU and ZANU elements within its ranks. Despite the attempts of the presidents of the Frontline States to unite the nationalist movements under the umbrella of a Muzorewa-led ANC in December 1974, the declaration of unity did not last long and was never fully implemented. From the beginning, ZANU could not accept Muzorewa's belief in a peaceful resolution of the Rhodesia problem, and ZAPU believed that Muzorewa was a mere 'caretaker' leader in the absence in detention of Nkomo and other senior politicians. No wonder then that when Muzorewa began to chart an independent political path, the ANC suffered splits as ZANU and ZAPU cadres withdrew, with those supporting Nkomo forming the African National Council-Zimbabwe (ANC-Z) and those supporting ZANU organising themselves into the People's Movement (PM).[150] ZANU went further by blocking Muzorewa's visit to ZANLA camps in Mozambique.

Members of ZANU and ZAPU, who were gradually imbibing Marxist-Leninist-Maoist ideologies, insinuated that the Christian religion was not a proper vehicle for the struggle against a colonialism that at times justified its legitimacy on Christian grounds. Muzorewa, as a bishop, was not considered an ideal person to lead the nationalist struggle that had already embraced the armed option. Muzorewa's deep religiosity and opposition to violence as an instrument of struggle further minimised his chances of acceptance by those who had resolved to liberate the country through armed struggle.[151]

Just like Sithole before him, Muzorewa was snubbed by other nationalists, particularly those in detention, who wanted to continue where they had left off in 1964. But Muzorewa had managed to build a political profile and support inside the country that sustained his United National African Council

149. Ibid., pp. 231–2.

150. *Zimbabwe Star*, December 1975.

151. Mufuka, 'Rhodesia's Internal Settlement', p. 440.

(UANC), which stood independent of the patronage and tutelage of ZAPU or ZANU. The UANC pursued the goal of peaceful negotiations with Ian Smith from 1977 onwards, culminating in the signing of the 3 March 1978 Agreement and the short-lived Zimbabwe-Rhodesia government with Muzorewa as prime minister.

Before situating the internal settlement in the broader issues of nationalism and the liberation struggle, it is important to sketch Muzorewa's nationalist vision as set out in his autobiography *Rise Up and Walk*, published in 1978. Just like Sithole, Muzorewa begins with his quest for education and the Christian God. When he joined active politics in 1972, Muzorewa emphasised unity through the slogan 'Unity is Power.'[152] A few weeks after successfully opposing the Smith-Home Proposals, Muzorewa was invited to speak by the Salisbury Chapter of the National Affairs Association. He took advantage of the invitation to advance his agenda of forging a nation under the theme 'Sound a Trumpet to Build a Heritage.' During his speech, he stated:

> We are not yet a nation, but we are struggling to be recognised as one people and one nation. If all of us show sufficient goodwill, and have enough mutual understanding of each other, we can become one nation for one people ... Let us not allow a poisonous spirit to engulf us as a nation. This could lead to bloodshed.[153]

Muzorewa did not hide the fact that he represented a moderate voice in African nationalist politics, emphasising that: 'Will this genuine hand of friendship extended by moderate Africans be refused? If so, one can only fear that this reasonable line of thinking, if not heeded by those in power, will be replaced by a more militant one.'[154]

On the question of the unity of all nationalist movements under the ANC with him as its president, Muzorewa blamed competition for leadership as the main source of division and the failure of all other initiatives to secure unity. Muzorewa also blamed and railed against tribalism as a spoiler in Zimbabwean nationalist politics. He noted that in a ZANU broadcast from Lusaka, a divisive line was maintained, to the extent that one speaker boasted that: 'If both Mr. Smith and Bishop Muzorewa were put before me, I would choose to shoot Muzorewa first before I shoot Ian Smith.' He added that:

> That kind of insanity derived both from a renascent tribalism and an insatiable lust for power. It was pathetic that these leaders spent their time scheming to have

152. A.T. Muzorewa, *Rise Up and Walk: An Autobiography* (London: Evans Brothers, 1978), p. 118.
153. Muzorewa, *Rise Up and Walk*, p. 122.
154. Ibid., p. 124.

> those of one particular tribe rule Zimbabwe while Zimbabweans of all tribes were suffering and dying to liberate their country.[155]

He commended FROLIZI leaders for taking unity more seriously than others. In his autobiography, Muzorewa makes it clear that he never supported violence of any sort. This is how he puts it:

> By nature I am a non-violent person. Since childhood I have recoiled at the sight of blood, and the presence of violent death. I have never been reconciled to the necessity of slaughtering animals for food. Physical suffering and pain always arouse strong emotions in me. I hold that all forms of life, even the lowliest, are sacred. Life, I believe, is God's greatest gift to the world, and should be valued as such. I believe also in the principle of non-violence ... Harmony in any society is preferable to violence. Even where pressures must be brought to bear on those in power to achieve greater justice, I would prefer using non-violent direct action, as did Mahatma Gandhi and Martin Luther King, Jr.
>
> Given a clear choice, all things being equal, I would by conviction adopt the non-violent means to settle any dispute. A settlement arrived at through peaceful negotiations, through give and take to achieve a mutual understanding, is far more stable than a settlement arising out of a test of force. The latter approach leaves a legacy of distrust on both sides, and feelings of injustice among the losers which become the seeds of future conflict. Violence breeds more violence. Violence easily becomes the precedent for settling disputes ... Knowing these facts, my preference for a non-violent approach to conflict is deep-seated.[156]

Despite these deep-seated convictions, Muzorewa ended up supporting the use of violence in the liberation struggle to maintain his legitimacy as a committed freedom fighter, while at the same time not closing the door to negotiations, unlike ZANU. This is how he put it:

> Zimbabweans have no other recourse but to pick up weapons and fight back. The Zimbabwe war of liberation is not an aggression against white people. It is a last response, taken in self-defence, when all non-violent methods have been tried and spurned by our oppressors. This is why I am a freedom fighter ... I cannot sit smugly and passively in the comfort of my house while my people are being tortured to death, shot down, or bombed.[157]

Muzorewa also made his ideas on the war crystal clear:

> I am no romantic concerning war, and the suffering and death which it entails. A liberation war is not for me an end in itself, but a means to an end of political liberation. I abhor the philosophy that prolonged war liberates the mind. This to

155. Ibid., p. 148.
156. Ibid., p. 175.
157. Ibid., p. 177.

> me is inhuman. War remains a last resort, to be employed as a form of self-defence when all other means to achieve justice have been tried in vain.[158]

This background is important to understanding the internal settlement, which so far has been excluded from mainstream narratives on nationalism and the liberation struggle. In Muzorewa's *Rise Up and Walk*, the last chapter is interestingly entitled 'Will a Free Zimbabwe be Truly Free?' and in it he poses some of the most challenging and honest questions:

> Will a free Zimbabwe be truly free?
> Will future generations accuse us of delivering to them a country whose independence is a fraud, a sham, a hollow shell? Will ours be called a 'free state', but in fact be mortgaged heavily to external international interests? Will we of Zimbabwe stand in danger of being satisfied, yes even thrilled, with the mere trappings of independence – a brand new flag fluttering in the breeze, sleek and shiny limousines, and black faces in Parliament, State House, the OAU and the United Nations – while those in power are not accountable to the governed for their actions? We who are directly involved in the struggle for Zimbabwe's independence owe it to future generations to keep on asking these questions. We must dedicate ourselves to achieve for Zimbabwe genuine independence.[159]

In popular and mainstream nationalist narratives, Muzorewa and Sithole are ignored as sell-outs and puppets who compromised with Ian Smith to produce false independence. No one has deconstructed this portrayal popularised by those nationalists in the Patriotic Front who favoured the violent armed struggle as the only liberation option. The Internal Settlement is given as a clear example of selling-out by Muzorewa and Sithole.

Is this a fair assessment of this settlement? David Chanaiwa has argued that the nationalist liberation struggle in Zimbabwe was, per se, characterised by the politics of competition for leadership, factionalism, power struggles, and political alliances of convenience and deals rather than by genuine ideological differences.[160] The struggle was not only against colonialism, but pitched some nationalists against others. This is what Masipula Sithole has analysed and defined as *struggles within the struggle*.[161] Having a different vision for achieving independence created enemies. There was also the deliberate and consistent elbowing-out of some nationalists and assassination of others, as the nationalist revolution ate its own children. This intolerant spirit was well represented by Dumiso Dabengwa's statement in 1961 when he proclaimed that 'any African who remains independent and does not take part in the common cause is as

158. Ibid., p. 215.
159. Ibid., pp. 241–2.
160. Chanaiwa, 'Zimbabwe: Internal Settlement in Historical Perspective', p. 76.
161. Sithole, *Zimbabwe: Struggles within the Struggle: Second Edition.*

bad and as sell-out as the so called moderates ... Those who are not with us are against us.'[162]

The intolerance towards moderates like Muzorewa, rather than substantive analysis of the Internal Settlement, earned him the label of sell-out. Instead of the Internal Settlement representing a deliberate betrayal of the national liberation struggle, it reflected the culmination of continuous struggles among leading nationalist actors, who by 1977 had grouped themselves uneasily into various internal 'governments-in-waiting' and 'governments-in-exile.'[163] Looked at closely, the settlement embodied the realisation of the major objectives of the broader nationalist struggle. As argued by Ndabaningi Sithole: 'The internal African nationalist leaders succeeded where all others had failed.' He added that:

> The Agreement ensures that Zimbabwe will become independent on 31 December 1978 on the firm foundation of the democratic principle of majority rule based on one man one vote. In effect it represents the end of white rule and the beginning of black rule in Zimbabwe, and is therefore rightly regarded as the most significant event in the country's history.[164]

Like all negotiated settlements, it was not perfect. There is always give and take in such negotiations. Evaluated in the context of a colonial settler society, with its extensive culture of dominating Africans, the settlement surpassed all other previous negotiations. It included majority rule, universal suffrage, non-racialism and a Bill of Rights.[165] The negotiations were protracted, stretching across three months. Measured in terms of the moderate nationalist positions of Muzorewa and Sithole, founded on African bourgeois ideologies of legitimation, it was a great achievement. Measured also against Ian Smith's vow that there was not going to be majority rule in a thousand years, it was a great African stride.

Evaluations of the success of the Internal Settlement must also be measured against the reality of a UANC dominated by African intellectuals with high educational achievements but constrained in accumulating wealth by colonial racism.[166] Thus, the Internal Settlement can be understood as a class project pushed by moderate intellectuals such as Dr. Ernest Bulle, Professor Stanlake Samkange, Dr. Joseph Kamsikiri, and many others who were not enamoured of Marxist-Leninist-Maoist political philosophies. When Stanlake Samkange and his wife Tommie Marie Samkange wrote *Hunhuism or Ubuntuism: A Zimbabwe*

162. *Bantu Mirror*, 6 May 1961.
163. Ndlovu-Gatsheni. 'Puppets or Patriots', p. 368.
164. Sithole, *In Defence of the Rhodesia Constitutional Agreement*, p. 8.
165. Rhodesian Government, *Rhodesian Constitutional Agreement, 3rd March 1978, No. 44* (Salisbury: Government Printer, 1978).
166. J. Ngara, 'The Zimbabwe Revolution and the Internal Settlement', in *Marxism Today* (November 1978), p. 343. See also A.K.H. Weinrich, *Black and White Elites in Rural Rhodesia* (Manchester: Manchester University Press, 1973).

Political Philosophy, they were trying to undercut the appeal of the Marxism-Leninism-Maoism of ZAPU and ZANU.[167] As they put it:

> There is an indigenous philosophy deeply imbedded in the past and inextricably interwoven with our culture that we can call hunhuism or ubuntuism. Hunhuism or ubuntuism permeates and radiates though facets of our lives, such as religion, politics, economics etc. Some aspects of hunhuism or ubuntuism are applicable to the present and future as they were in the past. It is not necessary for Africans to swallow, holus-bolus foreign ideologies more suited to foreign people and foreign lands.[168]

To those intellectuals supporting the Internal Settlement, it was the best deal crafted by internal people without foreign ideologies. ZANU and ZAPU were dismissed as consumers of such ideologies, which were not consonant with the ideology of Zimbabwe-Rhodesia, founded on the mobilisation of indigenous political philosophy.

But the Internal Settlement had contentious features that helped its enemies easily dismiss it as a sell-out. The first was the double-barrel name of the country – Zimbabwe-Rhodesia instead of merely Zimbabwe, as the nation was imagined by nationalists. The second was the sharing of ministerial positions through co-ministers, which gave the impression of political power- and authority-sharing between coloniser and colonised. The third issue was the continuation of the white-dominated parliament during the transitional period. The fourth issue was the reserved white seats that contradicted the principles of majority rule and non-racialism, and that entrenched white separate representation. But both Sithole and Muzorewa railed against racial representation, arguing that it 'smacks of discrimination in an independent African state based on one man one vote' and maintained 'an independent European community in an independent African state.'[169]

The woes of the Internal Settlement were exacerbated by its failure to bring an end to the liberation war and to gain international acceptability as a legitimate decolonisation package. However, it was not very different from the other negotiated compromise settlements that brought about transfer of power from whites to blacks in Africa.

By examining the autobiography of Muzorewa we also gain some insight into his vision for a postcolonial state and the character of its leadership. Exploring the question of 'Will a Free Zimbabwe be Truly Free?' Muzorewa engaged with the stubborn questions of neocolonialism, the nature of freedom, ideology, land,

167. S. Samkange and T.M. Samkange, *Hunhuism or Ubuntuism: A Zimbabwe Indigenous Political Philosophy* (Salisbury: Graham Publishing, 1980).
168. Ibid., p. 103.
169. *The Zimbabwe Times*, 28 March 1978.

sovereignty, leadership and national unity. Basing his vision for the future on observations and studies of what was happening in those countries that gained independence ahead of Zimbabwe, he isolated key issues that Zimbabwe had to avoid. In the first place, he posed the question of what had been learnt from other parts of Africa and his response was:

> We have seen states emerging as happy, prosperous dominions at independence only to fall into the grip of local tyrants who treat the state as their own fiefdom. We have seen states emerge as 'independent' but owing their independence to some external country which then proceeds to hold them to ransom – the former ally overstaying her welcome and exploiting the people's wealth. We have seen states emerge at independence as rich, self-sufficient entities but later become poverty-stricken 'banana republics' through frivolous spending, laziness, and maladministration. I have come across independent peoples who rue the day they obtained political freedom, who furtively wish that the former colonizers were back.[170]

Muzorewa engaged with the question of: 'What type of freedom do we wish for Zimbabwe?' His response was that 'Zimbabweans want no counterfeit freedom. No second-rate independence, no worn-out ideologies.' To him, genuine freedom entailed three qualities of political life: 'freedom from outside control, the sovereignty of the people, and self-determination of the nation's political and economic destiny.'[171]

Ideologically, Muzorewa railed against foreign ideologies, including foreign economic systems, in favour of what he termed 'national ideology' based on the particular circumstances of a particular people and society.[172] On land, Muzorewa stated that it was the major resource of Zimbabwe and that it needed to be made available to the people on an equal basis. He argued that:

> I accept that land is too valuable a resource for its distribution to be determined by purely political considerations. I accept that land distribution or redistribution must be largely guided by economic considerations because I subscribe to the view that land is primarily for production and must continue to be a viable and not a wasting resource.[173]

Muzorewa engaged with the crucial issue of leadership in Zimbabwe and delineated the qualities and virtues of a good leader in this way:

> If Zimbabwe is to be truly free and liberated, the head of the state must be a liberated person himself. He must be free from the shackles of evil deeds or an evil

170. Muzorewa, *Rise Up and Walk*, p. 242.
171. Ibid., p. 242.
172. Ibid., p. 244.
173. Ibid., p. 248.

> past which would catch up with him. He must be liberated from the constraints of tribalism and racism. He must be an ordinary person – not one infatuated by his own sense of self-importance. Zimbabwe needs as a political head a man or woman capable of love, for the nation is going to need a great deal of loving after 100 years of burning hate.[174]

Muzorewa also stated that the ideal Zimbabwean head of state must be a mature person who knows that he/she is not God; must be open to criticism, accommodating critics and friends alike; be a secure and confident person immune to seeing plots behind every bush and to inventing plotters to execute or harass; rise above racism and tribalism; be a nation-builder able to weld races and tribes into one nation; and be an able administrator and manager.[175] Finally, Muzorewa raised the issue of whether Zimbabwe would find a workable succession formula. His vision was captured in these words:

> I want to see the day when Zimbabwe will remove a head of state democratically. I want to see an elder statesman gracefully step down and settle down to private life or to some other public office without becoming the focal point for rebellion against the new leadership.[176]

To him, a truly free Zimbabwe would be the product of efforts to build one nation, to stamp out racism and tribalism and to inaugurate reconciliation and harmony. Reading these insights of Muzorewa led me to reconsider the views of those who labelled him a puppet, a traitor and a sell-out without necessarily according him the status of political saint.

But it is important to emphasise that, as with all politicians, Sithole's and Muzorewa's political rhetoric and writings did not always match their political practices even during the short-lived Zimbabwe-Rhodesia era. Sithole accused Muzorewa's supporters of using violence in the run-up to the elections that resulted in the Zimbabwe-Rhodesia government. Sithole further complained that the elections were not free and fair. As the first black transitional prime minister, Muzorewa was accused by both ZAPU and ZANU of authorising the bombings of rear bases in Zambia and Mozambique.

174. Ibid., p. 256.
175. Ibid.
176. Ibid., p. 157.

6. Transition and Postcolonial Crisis

What has often been ignored in the analysis of Zimbabwean postcolonial politics is the unique ideological circumstances of its birth in 1980. Zimbabwe joined the community of African nations as the 50th independent state on 18 April 1980. Among its unique features was that it was neither an 'early decoloniser' of the 1960s nor a 'late decoloniser' of the 1990s. It was a 'mid-decoloniser.' This meant that the young state stood uneasily astride the fading socialist world and the emerging neoliberal world that had not yet become triumphant.

At birth, the young state was forced to dream in both socialist and liberal terms. Its political ideology was captive to these antagonistic worlds. Added to this was the fact that the transfer of political power from the white settler political elite to the black nationalist elite took the form of negotiated settlement at Lancaster House in Britain under the supervision of Britain and America. One of the duties of the Western patrons was to make sure those radical Marxist ideologies that had been imbibed by the liberation forces, and that advocated the total smashing of the colonially constructed state and the building of a new socialist republic did not materialise. At the end of decolonisation, Zimbabwe was born as a successor to the Rhodesian colonial state rather than as a new alternative to it.

Any serious analysis of the roots of the crisis of the NDR in Zimbabwe must be traced to the Lancaster House Settlement of 1979. The settlement was directly responsible for compromising a 'revolutionary' transition, under which racially biased inequalities in land and asset distribution could have been resolved. As argued in the earlier section of this study, a 'revolutionary' transition was also made remote by the dominance of the African elites like Joshua Nkomo, Robert Mugabe and many others, who had not completely 'committed class suicide' to fully embrace the radical demands of the peasants, workers and the fighting forces of ZIPRA and ZANLA, which desired radical changes. The African elite throughout Africa were mainly concerned with taking over where the white colonial bourgeoisie had left off as new leaders rather than with radical transformation. Worse still, the radical ZIPA cadres had been disciplined, killed and detained by the old-guard.[177] The failure of the Zimbabwean transition to assume a 'revolutionary' character has been well described as a 'revolution that

177. D. Moore, 'The Ideological Formation of the Zimbabwean Ruling Class,' in *Journal of Southern African Studies,* 17 (3) (September 1991), pp. 472–95; D. Moore, 'Democracy, Violence and Identity in the Zimbabwean War of Liberation: Reflections from the Realms of Dissent,' in *Canadian Journal of African Studies,* 29 (3) (December 1995); D. Moore, 'The Zimbabwe People's Army: Strategic Innovation or Moore of the Same? In N. Bhebe and T. Ranger (eds), *Soldiers in Zimbabwe's Liberation War* (London: James Currey, 1995), pp. 73–103, and T. Ranger, 'The Changing of the Old Guard: Robert Mugabe and the Revival of ZANU,' in *Journal of Southern African Studies*, 7 (1) (October 1980), pp. 71–90.

lost its way.'[178] Zimbabwe was therefore born with what Amanda Hammar and Brian Raftopoulos termed 'unfinished business.'[179] John Higley defined the 'revolutionary' model of transition as consisting of:

> ... [w]holesale change in both the composition and relations of elites. Not only political but also most state administrative, economic, military, media and professional elites are displaced by a doctrinaire counter-elite that wins a revolutionary struggle or that is imposed by an external power through military conquest. The newly ascendant counter-elite builds a sharply centralised and coercive regime aimed at transforming society to accord with its doctrinal precepts.[180]

While the transition to independence in Zimbabwe did not take an outright 'revolutionary' route, it did not fit well with what Higley has termed 'settlement,' in which:

> ... [t]here is not much change in the composition of elites, but established leaders of elite camps negotiate a sudden, deliberate, and relatively comprehensive 'settlement' involving compromises of core disputes. The result is a much more integrated set of elites whose competitions are more restrained and whose relations are more mutually accommodating. This lays the basis for a stable democratic regime.[181]

The Zimbabwean transition to independence took the form of a 'half-way house' between 'revolutionary' and 'settlement' patterns. Despite the limitations imposed by the Lancaster House Agreement and the Lancaster House Constitution, ZANU-PF, which had emerged triumphant in the elections of 1980, committed itself to carrying out some of the key tasks of the NDR. As mentioned in the opening section of this study, NDR in Zimbabwe has remained vaguely defined and ambiguously articulated across both ZAPU and ZANU nationalist political formations, compared, for instance, to South Africa's African National Congress.

However, Thabo Mbeki deployed the concept of NDR as articulated by the African National Congress and used it to evaluate the performance of ZANU-PF as a nationalist party and as the first black government of Zimbabwe. According to Mbeki, the first phase of the NDR was the struggle for independence itself and the second phase comprised attempts to meet popular demands and expectations of liberation. He summarised the tasks of ZANU-PF as:

178. A. Astrow, Zimbabwe: *A Revolution That Lost Its Way?* (London: Zed, 1983).

179. A. Hammar and B. Raftopoulos, 'Zimbabwe's Unfinished Business: Rethinking Land, State and Nation', in Hammar, Raftopoulos, and Jensen (eds), *Zimbabwe's Unfinished Business*, pp. 1–47.

180. J. Higley, 'Transitions and Elites', in A. Braun and Z. Barany (eds), *Dilemmas of Transition: The Hungarian Experience* (Boulder: Rowman and Littlefield, 1999), p. 48.

181. Ibid.

- Ending poverty and underdevelopment, especially among the formerly colonised masses.
- Bridging the disparities between the formerly colonised and the former colonisers in terms of wealth, income and opportunity and de-racialising the patterns of ownership of productive property.
- Ensuring that the economy grows and develops in a manner that can sustain the two objectives above.
- Further entrenching democracy by ensuring the greater involvement of the masses of the people in the system of governance, while ensuring the continued allegiance of the masses of the people to the party of the revolution.
- Securing Zimbabwe's rightful place in Southern Africa, Africa and the rest of the world, bearing in mind the objective circumstances brought about by the process of globalisation.[182]

This was of course not the Zimbabwean or ZANU-PF rendering of NDR. Mbeki was drawing on the African National Congress's version of NDR and applying it seamlessly to ZANU-PF and Zimbabwe. The ZANU-PF rendition of NDR is commonly linked to the concept of *Chimurenga* (a Shona word meaning nationalist resistance and nationalist revolution). According to ZANU-PF, the Zimbabwean nationalist revolutionary history unfolded in terms of three *Chimurengas* (*Zvimurenga*): *First Chimurenga* (1896–97); *Second Chimurenga* (1960s-70s) and *Third Chimurenga* (1997–2003).[183] Beyond fighting for political independence, sometimes simplistically defined as African conquest of white settlers, NDR in Zimbabwe remained vague on issues of democracy and human rights. Social justice was reduced to land reform involving taking land from white commercial farmers to give to black people.

There is no doubt that ZANU-PF, under the leadership of Mugabe, demonstrated revolutionary consistency during the first phase of the NDR. This involved two cardinal tasks. The first was prosecuting national liberation from foreign and white settler minority rule, and the second was the establishment of an independent and democratic state. However, this positive evaluation of ZANU-PF's and Mugabe's role in the first phase of NDR often ignores the scope of democratic practice within the liberation movement project that had a bearing on future approaches to issues of democracy and human rights. This is

182. T. Mbeki, 'A Discussion Document: The Mbeki-Mugabe Papers: What Mbeki Told Mugabe', August 2001. The first phase of the NDR is here defined as the struggle for national liberation from foreign rule and white minority rule.

183. T. Ranger, 'Nationalist Historiography, Patriotic History and the History of the Nation: The Struggle Over the Past in Zimbabwe,' in *Journal of Southern African Studies*, 30 (2) (June 2004), pp. 215–34. See also S.J. Ndlovu-Gatsheni, 'Making Sense of Mugabeism in Local and Global Politics: 'So Blair Keep Your England and Let Me Keep My Zimbabwe,' in *Third World Quarterly*, 30 (6) (2006), pp. 1139–58.

how John S. Saul posed this challenge: 'Let us interrogate first the democratic dimension: in sum, liberation for whom?' He added:

> The various liberation movements in southern Africa claimed, as did anti-colonial nationalist movements elsewhere, to speak in the name of the masses of their oppressed populations and at one level there was truth to this: the drive to remove the structures of white minority rule was certainly a liberatory one. But was this to be seen, paradoxically, as being primarily a case of 'liberation without democracy?' ... Was there a range of significant variation between the practices of different liberation movements across southern Africa in this respect? And what have been the implications for post-liberation politics of the wedge which was always liable to be forced open between 'liberation' and 'democracy' in the course of the region's war, to go no further afield.[184]

For ZANU-PF, democratic and human rights questions provided the necessary resources for rhetoric and propaganda as it mobilised colonised people across class and ethnic divisions. Claude Ake had this to say about how nationalists constantly harked back to the issue of democracy:

> The language of the nationalist movement was the language of democracy, as is clear from: *I speak of Freedom* (Nyerere), *Without Bitterness* (Orizu), *Facing Mount Kenya* (Kenyatta), *Not Yet Uhuru* (Odinga), *Freedom and Development* (Nyerere), *African Socialism* (Senghor), and *The Wretched of the Earth* (Fanon). It denounced the violation of dignity of the colonised, the denial of basic rights, the political disenfranchisement of the colonised, racial discrimination, lack of equal opportunity and equal access, and economic exploitation of the colonised. The people were mobilised according to these grievances and expectations of a more democratic dispensation.[185]

Towards the beginning of the 2000s, the nationalist project represented by ZANU-PF continued to degenerate and shed its progressive aspects. There are a number of indicators that demonstrate this regression. First was the consolidation of an 'imperial presidency,' together with the spreading of the personality cult of Robert Mugabe as the embodiment of state and nation. The second development was increasing deployment of violence and coercion as a mode of governance. Third was incremental closure of democratic spaces through tightening repression. The fourth development was the appearance of the war veterans and the nationalist leaders as the 'first citizens' of the nation, to whom all other people were expected to pay homage as the liberators of Zimbabwe. This development happened in tandem with the militarisation of state institutions and in-

184. J.S. Saul, *Decolonisation and Empire: Contesting the Rhetoric and Reality of Resurbordination in Southern Africa and Beyond* (Wales and Johannesburg: Merlin Press and Wits University Press, 2008), p. 50.
185. C. Ake, *The Feasibility of Democracy in Africa* (Dakar: CODESRIA, 2000), p. 46.

creasing executive lawlessness. All this combined to make democracy an orphan in Zimbabwe. Ranger mounted one of the most robust critiques of the character of Zimbabwean nationalism by arguing that the nationalist liberation wars had proven to be fertile ground for the development of authoritarianism, personality cults, commandism and violence, where 'disagreement could mean death.'[186]

It must be noted that ZANU originally emerged in circumstances marked by violence from both the intransigent colonial settler state and from the ZAPU it had split from in 1963. The intransigence and bellicosity of the Rhodesia settler state also forced both ZAPU and ZANU into militancy and to embrace violence as a legitimate tool of liberation. On this development, John Makumbe has argued that 'supposedly democratic political parties, formed for the twin purposes of putting an end to colonialism and creating a democratic dispensation in Zimbabwe, were forced to become militant and militaristic liberation movements.'[187] Both ZAPU and ZANU received military support from the former Soviet Union, Eastern Europe, Cuba, and China, in addition to the support of fellow Africans on the continent. Thus, the Socialist bloc had a lasting impact on the liberation movements to the extent that 'the political organisation of ZANU … assumed the eastern bloc format, complete with a central committee and politburo.'[188]

The conduct of the armed struggle against a belligerent settler state gave rise to a number of developments that left a lasting impression on ZANU-PF and the state it created in 1980. The first was militarisation of the liberation movement, together with the development of commandist and regimental attributes. The second was the prominence of the party leader within the movement, which gradually evolved into a personality cult. The third was that the militarist approach tended to brook no dissent. The fourth was the building of a nationalist-military alliance that has survived until today, in terms of which top army commanders are loyal ZANU-PF members.[189] The final aspect was the development of a culture of violence as a legitimate tool for achieving political goals (e.g., 'the ZANU axe must continue to fall upon the necks of rebels when we find it no longer possible to persuade them into the harmony that binds us all,' and Mugabe's 'degrees in violence' speech).[190]

Makumbe argued that these developments implied that ZANU 'would be-

186. Ranger, 'Leaving Africa: Making and Writing History in Zimbabwe'.

187. Makumbe, 'ZANU-PF: A Party in Transition', p. 34.

188. Ibid.

189. Ndlovu-Gatsheni, 'Nationalist-Military Alliance and the Fate of Democracy in Zimbabwe', pp. 49–80.

190. A number of studies contain quotations from ZANU-PF politicians and Mugabe regarding their proclivity for violence. See Blair, *Degrees in Violence;* M. Meredith, *Our Votes, Our Guns: Robert Mugabe and the Tragedy of Zimbabwe* (New York: Public Affairs, 2002); and Chan, *Robert Mugabe: Life of Power and Violence.*

come vulnerable to tendencies of authoritarianism and personalised rule.'[191] Under the influence of Eastern bloc countries that had one-party political systems, ZANU's pronouncements and propaganda throughout the liberation period into the 1980s and early 1990s emphasised the need to create a one-party socialist state in Zimbabwe.[192] Even today, ZANU-PF conducts itself politically as if Zimbabwe is under a one party-state political system. Makumbe further argued that ZANU-PF's adherence to socialist party organisational structures and systems of management has resulted in its failure to transform itself into a democratic political party, concluding that:

> The genesis of a political party seems to have a bearing on that party's future development. The Zimbabwe case seems to illustrate that liberation movements struggle to transform themselves into democratic political parties when their countries become liberated or independent. Indeed, whenever they are threatened with loss of political power, former liberation movements tend to resuscitate their original achievements as liberators as a licence to continued tenure of office. They also harness their wartime tactics of instilling fear in the electorate to win elections.[193]

This analysis is very useful in understanding the current political behaviour of ZANU-PF and Mugabe in relation to opposition politics and issues of constitutionalism, democracy and human rights. What has become clear is that this tradition makes it very difficult to unseat those political parties with liberation roots, as they do not respect democratic principles when it comes to relinquishing power. Makumbe argue that 'indeed, it would be conceptually inconsistent for Mugabe to have been defeated at the polls. It takes undemocratic means to oust fully-fledged dictators.'[194] To its opponents, ZANU-PF, with its Stalinist tendencies, represents an old nationalism. The major characteristic of ZANU-PF politics is the pervasive belief that the movement knows what the people want, that the people owe their freedom from colonialism to it, that it has earned the right to rule Zimbabwe, in perpetuity, based on its tendency to privilege the 'political kingdom' over legalism and constitutionalism.[195]

However, there is no doubt that ZANU-PF and Mugabe, during his first years in office, indicated a move in the direction of a successful transitional and

191. Makumbe, 'ZANU-PF: A Party in Transition?', p. 34.
192. See I. Mandaza and L. Sachikonye (eds), *The One Party State and Democracy: The Zimbabwe Debate* (Harare: SAPES Books, 1991); and W.C. Reed, 'International Politics and National Liberation: ZANU and the Politics of Contested Sovereignty in Zimbabwe', in *African Studies Review*, 36 (2) (September 1993), pp. 31–59.
193. Makumbe, 'ZANU-PF: A Party in Transition?', p. 35.
194. Ibid., p. 39.
195. S.J. Ndlovu-Gatsheni, 'Reaping the Bitter Fruits of Stalinist Tendencies in Zimbabwe', *African Concerned Scholars Bulletin: Special Issue on the 2008 Zimbabwe Elections*, No. 79 (Spring 2008), pp. 21–31.

developmental state. However, the main flaw in the early economic and developmental policies was their dependence on redistribution of what was available without clear strategies for increasing production.[196] The early policies were geared towards large expenditures on education, health and welfare and rural development; subsidisation of essential commodities such as food and fuel; subsidisation of state corporations to keep the prices of the goods and services they supplied down; training and deployment of black Zimbabweans in senior positions in all areas of the public sector; upward adjustment of wages and salaries in the public sector to bridge the gap between black and white earnings; and a limited programme to encourage the emergence of a black rural and urban petit bourgeoisie.[197]

The second flaw was the failure to harmonise efforts of the private and public sectors in addressing poverty and underdevelopment. The private sector remained a sacred cow and the domain of the small but economically powerful white bourgeoisie, and played a minimal role in bridging the material disparities between the black and white communities.[198] This was partly due to ZANU-PF's surprisingly religious adherence to the Lancaster House Agreement's 'sunset clauses' in the economic arena, even as the movement violated its human rights and democratic clauses willy-nilly.[199]

What was immediately poignant was that the 'economy and the national budget could not carry the costs imposed on it by the requirement to respond to two of the tasks [ending poverty and underdevelopment] of the Second Phase of the National Democratic Revolution, of meeting the needs of the people.'[200] The only way out was to increase borrowing and to turn to international financial organisations such as the IMF for assistance. This resulted in the accumulation of debt by the young postcolonial state. While all this was happening, the ZANU-PF government 'maintained a complex system of government controls over the economy, which increased the cost of doing business in Zimbabwe and acted as a disincentive for investors who had the choice to invest in less regulated markets.[201]

The postcolonial Zimbabwean state, as an aspiring democratic developmental state, failed (economically) from the beginning as ZANU-PF 'adopted a subjective approach to the accomplishment of two tasks of the second phase of the

196. Davies, 'Memories of Underdevelopment: A Personal Interpretation of Zimbabwe's Economic Decline', pp. 19–41.

197. R.T. Libby, 'Development Strategies and Political Division within the Zimbabwean State', in M. Schartzberg (ed.), *The Political Economy of Zimbabwe* (New York: Praeger, 1984).

198. Discussion Document: The Mbeki-Mugabe Papers: What Mbeki Told Mugabe, August 2001.

199. See Mandaza (ed.), Zimbabwe: *The Political Economy of Transition.*

200. Discussion Document: The Mbeki-Mugabe Papers, p. 6.

201. Ibid.

NDR. In pursuing these tasks, it did not take into account the objective reality of fiscal and economic constraints.[202] By the late 1980s, the state ran out of resources, even though it had already appealed to the IMF for financial help from as early as 1984.[203] Thus, a subjective approach to the economy, which was solely driven by the populist desire to serve the interests of the ordinary masses, 'in the end … has imposed new and heavy burdens on the masses.'[204]

This situation was compounded by the failure of ZANU-PF to prevent the rise of cronyism, clientilism and corruption, which resulted in those close to the ruling party dividing up the national cake among themselves at the expense of the masses. George B.N. Ayittey argued that 'Africa's postcolonial development effort may be described as one giant false start,' with African leaders (with few exceptions) adopting the wrong political systems, such as 'sultanism' or one-party states; the wrong economic system (statism); the wrong ideology (socialism); and taking the wrong path (industrialisation via import substitution). He added that most leaders were functionally illiterate and given to schizophrenic posturing and sloganeering. The leadership lacked basic understanding of the development process.[205]

The ZANU-PF elite could be said to have proven over time to be 'functionally illiterate' when it came to the economy. This weakness in ZANU-PF led Mbeki to conclude that 'it is therefore imperative that the party of revolution of Zimbabwe should have a thorough understanding of economic questions in general and the Zimbabwe economy.'[206] The task of the national democratic state was misunderstood by ZANU-PF leaders simply to mean redistribution of wealth, and blaming colonialism for every failure in postcolonial Africa.

However, the ZANU-PF leadership has been severely criticised for failure to install democracy in Zimbabwe by an array of civil society organisations and opposition forces at home, as well as by the international community abroad. At independence, ZANU-PF was more concerned with devising ways to retain power and ensure regime security. Regime security concerns were privileged over opening up democratic spaces. To some extent security concerns were justified because of the threat of destabilisation by the apartheid regime and the disunity within the elite of the 1980s that culminated in the deployment of the Fifth Brigade to Matabeleland and the Midlands.

ZANU-PF adopted a number of strategies to safeguard regime security. The first was intolerance of opposition that manifested itself in the violent elimina-

202. Ibid., p. 10.
203. Dashwood, Zimbabwe: *The Political Economy of Transition.*
204. Discussion Document: The Mbeki-Mugabe Papers, p. 11.
205. G.B.N. Ayittey, *Africa Unchained: The Blueprint for Africa's Future* (New York: Palgrave Mcmillan, 2005), pp. 91–2.
206. Discussion Document: The Mbeki-Mugabe Papers, p. 13.

tion of PF-ZAPU as the first credible postcolonial opposition in Zimbabwe. The second was the increasing calls for a one-party state. The justifications for such calls included the question of economic development that was said to need monolithic unity; African tradition that was said to provide no space for opposition parties; and the idea that a multi-party system was not just a luxury in Africa but that it promoted the instability, regionalism and ethnicity that were obstacles to nation-building. Mugabe's speeches envisioned 'one state with one society, one nation, one party, one leader.'[207] He emphasised that as an indication of the unity of the people in Zimbabwe, 'they should be one party, with one government and one Prime Minister.'[208] This rhetoric of unity was used to destroy any prospect of pluralism within society and to drive societal demobilisation.[209]

As the national cake continued to shrink in the 1990s, the ZANU-PF government responded with increasing closures of democratic spaces coupled with the use of violence against those considered opponents. There were also noticeable changes in ZANU-PF's conception of nationalism, democracy and economic development. Sarah Rich Dorman claimed that 'the joint nation and party-building ... was defined in terms of three interlocking concepts: reconciliation and unity; development; and nationalist rhetoric and symbolism.'[210] She added that 'the regime's new legislative and security powers based upon the oppressive laws of the Rhodesian state, allowed it to regulate widely providing a political-military framework through which to dominate and demobilise society.'[211]

Norbert Tengende reinforced Dorman's analysis, arguing that the ZANU-PF nation-building project was nothing but an instrument of domination and control marked by the marginalisation of popular participation.[212] The tree of democracy was easily uprooted and substituted by the tree of presidentialism in the late 1980s. This was symbolically represented by what Dorman termed 'the omni-present "official portrait" of the president' that even substituted nationalism.[213] The year 1987 saw the establishment of the 'imperial executive presidency,' with Robert Mugabe as the incumbent, and the inauguration of 'the

207. *Moto Magazine*, 1 (4) (August 1982).

208. *Chronicle*, 25 January 1982.

209. C. Sylvester, 'Zimbabwe's 1985 Elections: A Search for National Mythology', *Journal of Modern African Studies*, 24 (1) (1986), p. 246.

210. S.R. Dorman, 'Inclusion and Exclusion: NGOs and Politics in Zimbabwe' (unpublished DPhil, University of Oxford, 2001), p. 50.

211. Ibid.

212. N. Tengende, 'Workers, Students and the Struggles for Democracy: State–Civil Society Relations in Zimbabwe' (unpublished PhD thesis, Roskilde University, 1994), p. 153. See also L. Sachikonye, 'The National-State and Conflict in Zimbabwe', in L. Laakso and A. Olokoshi (eds), *Challenges to the Nation-State in Africa* (Uppsala: Nordic Africa Institute, 1996), p. 142.

213. Dorman, 'Inclusion and Exclusion', p. 57.

father of the nation motif,' backed by liberation war credentials and nationalist iconography that is proving very hard to transcend democratically.

The 1990s saw not only the Economic Structural Adjustment Programme (ESAP) and the socioeconomic and political problems it generated, but also a struggle to recapture and defend the remaining democratic spaces by such groups as students, intellectuals and workers. The activists' mode of communicating was either by congregating into vocal civil society organisations like the Zimbabwe Congress of Trade Unions (ZCTU), Zimbabwe National Students Union (ZINASU), the National Constitutional Assembly (NCA), and many other issues-based NGOs, or displaying apathy towards national events and party activities, including non-participation in national elections.[214] This indicated 'disillusionment with the party of revolution.'[215] By 2000, it was clear that much of the population of Zimbabwe had lost confidence in ZANU-PF, as was partly revealed in the results of the parliamentary elections of that year, in which the newly formed MDC gained 57 seats.

The MDC had won support across racial, ethnic, gender, class and religious divides through its promised commitment to restore democracy, human rights, constitutionalism, the rule of law and economic sanity. These were issues ZANU-PF had downplayed in its political agenda.[216] It confronted issues of democracy only through its politics aimed at redressing colonial material and social injustices. These claims were quickly undermined by elite accumulation of land ahead of peasants and workers, together with state-sanctioned violence against both.[217]

Over the years, membership of ZANU-PF and support for Mugabe had become preconditions for access to employment, resources and authority. This happened in tandem with the loss of support among sections of the population that did not benefit from the political patronage and matronage. Worse still, as this process evolved, the structures of the party showed signs of atrophy, and the organisation began to deviate from its role as representing the popular will. The party was now perceived as the state abusing public resources and dispensing

214. Moyo, Makumbe, and Raftopoulos, *NGOs, the State and Politics in Zimbabwe.*

215. Discussion Document: The Mbeki-Mugabe Papers, p. 14.

216. M. Sithole, 'Zimbabwe's Eroding Authoritarianism', *Journal of Democracy*, 8 (1) (1997), pp. 127–41; and M. Sithole, 'Fighting Authoritarianism in Zimbabwe', *Journal of Democracy*, 12 (1) (2001).

217. *Politically Motivated Violence in Zimbabwe 2000–2001: A Report on the Campaign of Political Repression Conducted by the Zimbabwean Government Under the Guise of Carrying Out Land Reform* (Harare: Zimbabwe Human Rights NGO Forum, August 2001); and *Organised Violence and Torture in the June 2000 General Election in Zimbabwe: A Report Prepared by the Mashonaland Programme of the AMANI Trust* (Harare: AMANI Trust, 28 February 2002).

public resources to clients and cronies in a brazenly partisan and very destructive primitive-accumulation manner.[218]

Popular democracy found its way into intensive care and, in this context, such other agents as the war veterans, youth militias and the military have come to be the basis of ZANU-PF and Mugabe's power. While ZANU-PF thought it could control the war veterans, another development occurred, with a negative impact on the structures of the party:

> [T]he 'war veteran' structures are not subject to the processes of control and accountability binding the normal structures of the party of revolution. Accordingly, the 'war veterans' have achieved a level of autonomy that further weakens the capacity of the party of revolution to influence and lead the masses of the people. Because they are not bound by the practices of a normal party of revolution, the 'war veterans' resort to ways and means predicated on the use of force against the people, rather than the education and persuasion of these masses to support the revolutionary cause. For these reasons, they also attract into their ranks the lumpen proletariat in particular ... *Inevitably, therefore, to the extent that it sustains these parallel structures, the party of the revolution becomes an opponent of the democratic institutions of governance and democratic processes that it has itself established and encouraged and for whose establishment it fought most heroically, with many of its militants laying down their lives* [my emphasis].[219]

Having burst into Zimbabwe's body politic as the storm-troopers of ZANU-PF, the war veterans, in collusion with youth militias and 'militiarised' members of the national army, constituted themselves as extra-party and parallel political structures that were inimical to democracy, constitutionalism and the rule of law.

In 1980, Zimbabwe had emerged as one of the principal forces in African international relations, with Harare becoming a beehive of African diplomatic activity. Zimbabweans served in major leadership positions in the United Nations (UN), Commonwealth, Non-Aligned Movement (NAM) and Southern African Development Community (SADC). By 2000, this positive record was in danger of being destroyed.[220] As with its domestic policy, which struggled to grow beyond the constraints imposed on it by colonial and nationalist liberation tradition, foreign policy was also interpolated by ZANU-PF's tradition of liberation and locked within the inflexible prism of liberation and sovereignty. Throughout the liberation struggle, ZANU had borne the stigma of being an unwanted force, as 'the external environment which ZANU entered in 1964 was dominated by ZAPU.'[221] Thus ZANU had to struggle to find patrons. Its salvation came

218. Discussion Document: The Mbeki-Mugabe Papers, p. 18.
219. Ibid., p. 20.
220. Reed, 'International Politics and National Liberation', pp. 31–59.
221. Ibid., p. 36.

through the split in Sino-Soviet relations and it took advantage of China's own search for clients, which coincided with ZANU's search for patrons.[222]

This search for patrons and friends had an important impact on the development of ZANU's ideology and future mode of politics. ZANU found itself being embraced by Tanzania under Julius Nyerere, Ethiopia under Hail Mariam Mengistu, North Korea under Kim II Sung, Romania under Nicoli Ceausescu, Libya under Colonel Muammar Gaddafi and Yugoslavia under Joseph Tito.[223] However, ZANU-PF's victory in the 1980 elections and the statesman-like behaviour of Mugabe in the 1980s enabled ZANU-PF to gain more international friends, including in the Western democracies.

But by 1997, ZANU-PF began to pursue a very complicated foreign policy as it veered into Afro-radicalism and nativism at home and defaulted on foreign debt payments. Foreign policy became affected by the politics of stressed nationalism, grievance and resentment. This began with the official dropping of ESAP that had been imposed by the IMF with the complicity of some leading members of ZANU-PF's business and political elites. This was followed by consistent verbal attacks on the British and the Americans as imperialists bent on the recolonisation of Zimbabwe after the state's active intervention in the land question, and intervention in the Democratic Republic of Congo.[224]

A number of strategic and tactical issues were not seriously considered and had devastating effects on the economy. These included:

i. whether Zimbabwe had the capacity to confront and defeat the United Kingdom, considering this matter within the context of the global balance of forces and not only on the basis of the strength and commitment to principle of Zimbabwe's party of revolution;
ii. whether Zimbabwe was able to mobilise other forces globally, including the United Kingdom itself, to help her to achieve this objective;
iii. whether Zimbabwe was able to isolate the UK from its closest allies, these being the European Union and the United States of America;
iv. whether it was possible to persuade the developed world to contribute to the resolution of the land question in Zimbabwe, including honouring the 1998 pledges, in a situation in which the United Kingdom stood in opposition;
v. whether the conflict on this particular matter of the land was of such central importance that Zimbabwe was willing to sacrifice friendly relations with the developed world, affecting all other questions.[225]

---

222. Ibid., p. 40.
223. ZANU, 'ZANU in World Politics', *Zimbabwe Today*, 9 (18 April 1966); and ZANU, 'Diplomatic Struggle', *Zimbabwe News*, 10 (6) (November-December 1978).
224. Moyo and Yeros, 'Intervention: The Zimbabwe Question and the Two Lefts', p. 184.
225. Discussion Document: The Mbeki-Mugabe Papers, p. 23.

The fatal flaw in Zimbabwe's pursuit of an abrasive foreign policy towards the West is that it took place at the wrong time and the country had no capacity to contain its effects in the domestic sphere. Since the collapse of the Soviet Union and implosion of the socialist republics of eastern and central Europe, the developed capitalist world has assumed a hegemonic position in global economic and political affairs. Countries like China, Cuba and Vietnam gradually opened up to significant inflows of private capital from the developed capitalist world, while Zimbabwe went in the opposite direction of 'Looking East.' ZANU-PF and Mugabe miscalculated strategically and tactically, as it was clear that, 'at this historical moment, it is impossible to mobilise the disciplined socialist and anti-imperialist forces that it might have been possible to mobilise two decades ago, to act as a counterweight to the developed capitalist countries.'[226]

The fact that the country would end up in isolation, confronted by an array of international forces that could not be defeated outright eluded the ZANU-PF leadership. Zimbabwe also needed to work harder to avoid sinking into an ever-deepening social and economic malaise that would result in the reversal of many of the gains of the NDR.[227] By 2000, it was becoming clear that Zimbabwe was already falling faster into an ever-deepening social, economic and political crisis. Between 1997 and 2003, ZANU-PF presided over the burial of the national project through deliberate trammelling of people's basic human rights, choosing to govern through military operations and by promoting antipathy towards democracy and disdain for human rights. When one takes into account these negative realities, it becomes clear that Mbeki's appraisal of ZANU-PF as a 'party of revolution' was largely apologetic and somewhat supportive of the Mugabe regime. The opposition MDC consistently drew attention to Mbeki's sympathies towards ZANU-PF and Mugabe in his mediation of the Zimbabwe crisis. But eventually, Mbeki managed to convince both ZANU-PF and two MDC factions to sign a Global Political Agreement on 15 September 2008 that formed the basis for the establishment of an Inclusive Government in Zimbabwe. But the history of the fossilisation of the Zimbabwean nation-state project cannot be complete without a clear understanding of the role of the MDC, which has consistently sought to renew the national project through democratisation 'therapy' since its formation in September 1999.

226. Ibid., p. 24.
227. Ibid.

7. The MDC and Democratisation Therapy

Ever since its breakaway from ZAPU in 1963, ZANU, which in 1980 called itself ZANU-PF, has struggled to represent itself as the only authentic liberation movement and driver of the Zimbabwean national project. It has consistently delegitimated all other political parties, including ZAPU, as only providing perverted and false expressions of the national will, if not completely rubbishing other parties as counter-revolutionary formations, Trojan horses of external forces and puppets of forces inimical to the Zimbabwean nation-state project.[228]

Rosa Luxemburg posed the fundamental question that helps in understanding how ZANU-PF has continued to claim to be the embodiment of the Zimbabwean national project and to deny all other political formations any link with the nation-state project. 'Does there exist one political party which would not claim that it alone, among all others, truly expresses the will of the "nation" whereas all other parties give only perverted and false expressions of the national will?'[229] ZANU-PF represents this logic very well in Zimbabwe. But in September 1999, when the MDC was formed under the leadership of trade unionist Morgan Tsvangirai, a strong counter-political formation emerged that seriously challenged ZANU-PF's claims to be the only representative of the national will. The imagination and definition of the national project as expressed by ZANU-PF always reduced it to the liberation struggle and the land question at election times. This vision experienced a very rude jolt when MDC declared it exhausted and moribund for failing to accommodate the fundamental post-Cold War normative variables of democracy, human rights, social peace, human security, good governance and orderly management of the economy.[230]

Soon after its formation, MDC began to formulate a new alternative national project underpinned by the imperatives of good governance, democracy, human rights and empowerment of workers. The MDC also sought to set itself apart from ZANU-PF by embracing the traces of a post-nationalist politics founded on social movements rather than the tradition of nationalist liberation, which had been used to unleash personality cults, authoritarianism, cronyism and violence in Zimbabwe. In June 2000, Tsvangirai confidently located his party's project within post-nationalist terrain, openly declaring that:

228. S.J. Ndlovu-Gatsheni, 'Patriots, Puppets, Dissidents and the Politics of Inclusion and Exclusion in Contemporary Zimbabwe,' in *Eastern Africa Social Science Research Review*, XXIV (1) (January 2008), pp. 81–108.

229. Luxemburg, *The National Question*, p. 141.

230. B. Raftopoulos, 'The Labour Movement and the Emergence of Opposition Politics in Zimbabwe,' in B. Raftopoulos and L. Sachikonye (eds), *Striking Back: The Labour Movement and the Post-Colonial State in Zimbabwe, 1980–2000* (Harare: Weaver Press, 2001), pp. 1–24.

> In many ways, we are moving from the nationalist paradigm to politics grounded in civic society and social movements. It's like the role and influences that in South Africa, the labour movement and civil society organisations had over the African National Congress in the early 1990s. MDC politics are not nationalist inspired, because they focus more on empowerment and participation of the people. ZANU-PF's nationalist thinking has always been top-down, centralised, always trapped in a time warp. Nationalism was an end in itself instead of a means to an end. One of ZANU-PF's constant claims is that everyone in Zimbabwe owes the nationalist movement our freedom. It has therefore also become a nationalism based on patronage and cronyism.[231]

Tsvangirai and his MDC sought to imagine and construct a new national project that was imbued with the spirit of inclusion of all races, all ethnicities, as well as driven and propelled by the overarching desire to democratise Zimbabwe. This new national project, predicated on the ethos of good governance, was inspired by the unfolding of new struggles that advocated new politics grounded in 'basic-needs' and 'people-centred' development paradigms. It seems that the MDC was further encouraged by the global mood of possibilities that culminated in Francis Fukuyama declaring: 'The End of History and the Last Man.'[232] Michael Hardt and Antonio Negri also celebrated this age of political possibilities by claiming that 'the concept of national sovereignty is losing its effectiveness, so too is the so-called autonomy of the political.' [233] Developments in the Southern African region, particularly the rise of the Movement for Multiparty Democracy (MMD) in Zambia under a trade unionist, Frederick Chiluba, and its successful challenging of the nationalist-founded United National Independence Party (UNIP) under the veteran leader Kenneth Kaunda, may have given hope to MDC in its struggle against ZANU-PF.

The era was also dominated by numerous vocal grassroots social movements, celebrated by John S. Saul 'as a significant signpost on the road to a post-neoliberal and post-nationalist politics ... and as an impressive rallying point for those forces from below that might yet get things back on track in their country.'[234] These celebrations of politics grounded in social movements tended to ignore the continued resonance of nationalist sentiment in a post-Cold War Africa, with some social movements inspired by nationalism and advocating increased state intervention and more neo-Keynesian economic policies, rather than anti-state slogans and rhetoric.[235]

231. *Southern Africa Report*, 15 (3) (June 2000).
232. F. Fukuyama, *The End of History and the Last Man* (New York: Harper Collins, 1993).
233. M. Hardt and T. Negri, *Empire* (Cambridge: Harvard University Press, 2000), p. 305.
234. J. S. Saul, 'Starting from Scratch? A Reply to Jeremy Cronin', *Monthly Review*, 54 (7) (2002), 13.
235. Johnson, 'Whither Nationalism?', p. 3.

The key intellectual challenge is whether these indications of exhaustion of nationalism really opened possibilities for post-nationalist politics? Scholars like Mkandawire noted that nationalism defied its death and displayed a 'remarkably enduring resonance.'[236] Krista Johnson added that post-nationalism emerged as an ill-defined phenomenon that was used 'to characterise multiple and disparate political projects.' At one level, post-nationalism was used to connote a critique of post-independence state nationalism. At another level, it was deployed as a concept to explain a burgeoning socialist and anti-imperialist movement or sentiment. To liberal scholars, post-nationalism connoted a liberal democratic political project that placed emphasis on individual rights and multi-party politics. Radical Africanist and pan-Africanist scholars were generally wary of so-called post-nationalist political projects that were detached from the pan-African ideal and free of its moral imperatives. They viewed post-nationalism as promoting a more exclusionary and adversarial image of the nation.[237]

The advocates of the post-nationalist alternative in Zimbabwe tended to ignore the ability of nationalism to renew its agendas and projects. Throughout the 2000s, ZANU-PF mobilised enormous energy to revive nationalism as the authentic and pan-African progressive phenomenon. Within this revival, President Mugabe tried hard to portray himself as dedicated to the continuation of the historic mission of taking decolonisation to its logical end of economic decolonisation.

But Mkandawire argued that nationalism had always been double-sided, with virtues and darker aspects. Among its virtues were fostering a sense of community, patriotism and a sense of shared historical past. Its dark sides included promotion of strong communal feeling that could easily be turned into xenophobia, and emphasis on monolithic unity that could degenerate into undemocratic pressures for conformity and blind loyalty.[238] In Zimbabwe, ZANU-PF tried hard to reclaim the virtues of nationalism to counter a possible post-nationalist takeover.

The MDC projected a leaning towards a social democratic transformation agenda crafted within the neoliberal paradigm. It emphasised that a post-nationalist dispensation was claiming Zimbabwe for democracy, human rights, economic prosperity, constitutionalism and rule of law. But at its formation, it also tried to appropriate the liberation struggle as having been propelled by the working class. Gibson Sibanda, the founder deputy president of the MDC, argued that the political struggle in Zimbabwe was historically led by the working class and was fought for the dignity and sovereignty of the people. He noted that

236. Ibid.

237. Johnson, 'Whither Nationalism?', pp. 3–4.

238. T. Mkandawire, 'From Liberation Movements to Governments: On Political Culture in Southern Africa', *African Sociological Review*, 6 (1) (2002), pp. 12–13.

in the *First Chimurenga*, workers fought against exploitation in the mines, farms and industry, and peasants against the expropriation of their land. To him, the nationalist movement that led the *Second Chimurenga* was born out of, and built on, struggles of the working people. What then happened was that the current nationalist elite in ZANU-PF hijacked this struggle for its own ends, betraying the people's hopes and aspirations.[239]

The MDC did not seek to disparage the nationalist liberation tradition as a foundation myth of the postcolonial nation of Zimbabwe. Rather it sought to liberate the tradition from being monopolised by one political party as though it was not a national heritage of all Zimbabweans. To the MDC, the liberation struggle was made possible by the people of Zimbabwe, not by a few nationalist elites who continued to claim that they 'died' for all the people, that they liberated all the people. Their legitimacy was based on participation in the liberation struggle rather than election by the people of Zimbabwe. To the MDC, the nationalist revolution had been hijacked by power hungry nationalist elites as part of their claim to be the alpha and omega of the leadership of Zimbabwe. In a way, the post-nationalist discourse was not a negation of the liberation tradition by a rescue of the national project from abuse and betrayal of the people.[240] In a 2003 document on core values, goals and policy principles, the MDC recognized 'the struggle of the Zimbabwean people throughout our history for economic, social and political justice' and acknowledged 'the continuing liberation struggle for social, economic and political rights and freedoms.'[241]

Its 2008 policy documents projected the MDC as pursuing 'social liberation policies aimed at completing the unfinished business of the national liberation struggle and [it] shall strive for the democratic structural economic liberation, rehabilitation and transformation of Zimbabwe.'[242] Tsvangirai himself emphasized that the struggle in Zimbabwe had always been one for dignity and freedom, and that the workers and peasants were always in the forefront of the first and second liberation struggles that brought the country to independence and gave sovereignty to its people. What the MDC was fighting against was the evident fact that the ruling nationalist elite in ZANU-PF was exploiting this long history of struggle for its own ends.[243]

The MDC's 2005 manifesto for the parliamentary election portrayed the party as a non-racial and a 'truly national party that recognizes no ethnic, tribal,

239. MDC, *MDC Election Manifesto*, 2000.

240. Raftopoulos, 'The Labour Movement and the Emergence of Opposition Politics in Zimbabwe'.

241. MDC, 'From Crisis to Democratic Human-Centred Development: Values, Goals and Polices of the Movement for Democratic Change (MDC)', December 2003, p. 5.

242. MDC, *MDC Manifesto* (2008).

243. MDC, 'From Crisis to Democratic Human Centred Development', preface.

religious or racial boundaries. We offer the people a new Zimbabwe, a new beginning.'[244] As part of their agenda for delivering this 'new Zimbabwe' and a 'new beginning,' their goal was:

> A sovereign, democratic, prosperous and self-sufficient nation led by a compassionate government that respects the rule of law and the rights of all its people, pursuing their welfare and interests in an honest, transparent and equitable manner.[245]

The MDC's relentless emphasis on issues of democracy and human rights has forced ZANU-PF to fight to claim the democratic question as well. Recent speeches by both ZANU-PF and MDC following the elections of 29 March 2008 indicate how the issue of democracy and human rights has come to be the core issue in party politics in Zimbabwe. This politics is intertwined with the issue of land, food and jobs, with ZANU-PF emphasising land, and MDC jobs and food. Thus, following the victory of his party in the parliamentary elections, Tsvangirai issued a press statement in which he reiterated that in a 'New Zimbabwe' there would be restoration and not retribution; equality and not discrimination; love, not war; and tolerance, not hate. He portrayed the votes cast on Saturday 29 March 2008 as 'a vote for jobs; it was a vote for food, for dignity, for respect, for decency and equality, for tolerance, for love, and for trust.'[246]

Even the Global Political Agreement reflects the attempts to reach the middle ground in terms of ZANU-PF's and MDC's imagination of the national project. The dream of a new national project underpinned by a democratisation discourse represented by the MDC locked horns with a nationalist discourse represented by ZANU-PF that emphasised age-old opposition colonialism and espoused the politics of entitlement based on nativity. At the centre of the Inclusive Government that came into being on 11 February 2009 is the MDC, which continues to push for comprehensive democratisation of state structures, restoration of people's rights, security sector reform and a return of Zimbabwe to the international community of states on the one hand, and ZANU-PF hardliners, who are applying the brakes to change and democratisation and who are content with removal of so-called 'imperialist sanctions.'[247]

Like all compromise documents, the GPA as the foundation script for the new Inclusive Government in Harare could not escape vagueness on some of the crucial issues that have haunted the Zimbabwe nation-state project. In the first place, it remained vague on the crucial issue of transitional justice as a for-

244. MDC, *MDC Manifesto* (2005).
245. MDC, 'A New Zimbabwe, A New Beginning' (2007).
246. Morgan Tsvangirai, *Press Conference Statement*, 1 April 2008.
247. J. Smith-Hohn, 'Unpacking the Zimbabwe Crisis: A Situation Report,' in *Institute for Security Studies Situation Report*, 10 September 2009.

mal foundation for national healing, national reconciliation and national unity. While the MDC tried to push for a mechanism to make those who violated human rights accountable for their misdeeds, ZANU-PF favoured letting bygones be bygones for the sake of national stability. The GPA also failed to be explicit on security sector reform, despite overwhelming evidence of the securitisation of the state and the abuse of the state's security organs in resolving political power games.[248]

Thirdly, the land issue continues to be contentious, as there is no agreement on rationalising land reform policy.[249] The fourth contentious issue is that of sanctions removal. As noted by Judy Smith-Hohn, 'the decision to lift sanctions lies clearly with parties external to the agreement' but ZANU-PF expects MDC to lead the team in the removal of sanctions as if MDC was the one that invited them.[250] The other complication relates to the problematic sharing of executive powers between president and prime minister of the republic. This has recently provoked fears of the emergence of a 'government within a government' or the so-called parallel structures emerging in the prime minister's office, a prospect that has sent shock waves down the political spines of ZANU-PF hardliners opposed to change.[251]

The current status of the Zimbabwean nation-state project can therefore be best described as gridlock, in which the old represented by ZANU-PF are taking time to exit the political stage and the new represented by MDC are proving slow to be born. In the interregnum, monsters represented by the 'securocrats/military junta' in alliance with ZANU-PF hardliners are compounding the crisis of the nation-state project.

248. M. Rupiya, 'Zimbabwe: Governance through Military Operations,' in *African Security Review* 14 (3) (2005), pp. 117–18.

249. G. Ruswa, 'Solving the Zimbabwean Crisis: A Reflection on Land Reform in the Context of Political Settlement,' (Paper presented at the European Conference on African Studies of the Africa-Europe Group for Interdisciplinary Studies, Leipzig, Germany, 5 June 2009.

250. Smith-Hohn, 'Unpacking the Zimbabwe Crisis,' p. 4.

251. The lead vocalist is Jonathan Moyo whose political identity remains ambivalent and ambiguous within a terrain of politics in flux.

8. Conclusion: Is the Zimbabwe Crisis an African Crisis?

Like other nationalist-inspired national projects, Zimbabwe's arose as a response to the challenges imposed by colonialism. Inevitably, African nationalism became the nodal point around which the Zimbabwean nation-state project crystallised in the post-Second World War period. It was indeed the ubiquity of nationalism that led Terence Ranger, a leading student of Zimbabwean history, to argue that nationalist thought was too pervasive to be ignored as it ran through the long sequence of political thought from the proto-nationalism of the Bantu Congress of the 1940s and early 1950s through the revived mass nationalist parties of the 1960s and into guerrilla war. Ranger posited that interrogation of nationalist thought remains a crucial element in understanding contemporary debate about democracy in Zimbabwe.[252]

Since the mid-1990s, several developments in Zimbabwe have placed it in the media and academic spotlight. The most important one was the rise of what one would term the 'insurrection of nationalism.'[253] This took the form of the *Third Chimurenga* (a third war of liberation this time with a focus on economic empowerment via a fast-track land reform programme).[254] To those scholars like Sam Moyo and Paris Yeros, Zimbabwe was the only country at the end of the Cold War that was undergoing a revolution marked by a radical agrarian reform spearheaded by a radicalised state.[255] To these left-nationalist scholars, Zimbabwe became engaged in the complex process of taking the NDR forward through efforts to resolve delicate national and agrarian questions. These radical scholars wrote of a 'deep democracy' predicated on issues of social justice rather than electoralism and other liberal formalities that do not speak directly to people's material well-being and colonially induced mass injustices. This is how Moyo and Yeros saw the situation:

> If independence bequeathed a neo-colonial state in Zimbabwe, the late nineties saw a rebellion against neo-colonialism. There was an incipient radicalisation of the state from 1997 onwards marked by its interventionist role in the economy, the suspension of structural adjustment, and the listing of 1,471 farms for expropriation.[256]

252. T.O. Ranger, 'Leaving Africa: Making and Writing History of Zimbabwe,' (Harare, Zimbabwe: Valedictory Lecture, Monomotapa, Monomotapa Crown Plaza, 19 June 1997).
253. I.G. Shivji, 'The Rise, the Fall, and the Insurrection of Nationalism in Africa' (Paper presented as Keynote Address to CODESRIA East African Regional Conference, Addis Ababa, Ethiopia, 29–31 October 2003).
254. R.G. Mugabe, *Inside the Third Chimurenga: Our Land is Our Prosperity* (Harare: Government of Zimbabwe, 2001).
255. S. Moyo and P. Yeros, 'The Radicalised State: Zimbabwe's Interrupted Revolution,' in *Review of African Political Economy*, 111 (2007), pp. 103–21.
256. Ibid, p. 104.

The character of the Zimbabwean nation-state project as it unfolded during the early 2000s led to numerous intellectual interrogations that pitted left-leaning scholars, deploying political economy and class analysis, against liberal-minded scholars, concerned about issues of governance, human rights and democracy. The crisis has also fragmented the left-leaning camp into 'left-leaning nationalist scholars' and 'left-leaning internationalist scholars.' Moyo and Yeros defined themselves as 'left-leaning nationalist scholars' and they saw a 'revolutionary situation' unfolding in Zimbabwe under the *Third Chimurenga*. This was as 'a situation in which society is highly mobilised and in conflict, both among its socio-political formations and between them and the state.' In addition, this is a situation in which 'bourgeois institutions come under fundamental threat, in a progressive way.' 'In this context, property rights and formal democratic political norms and procedures (human rights) are either threatened or abrogated and basic bureaucratic structures and hierarchies are themselves threatened or suspended.'[257] In this line of thinking, the Zimbabwean nation-state project was an anti-neocolonialist phenomenon inspired by revived nationalist revolutionary force.

The internationally respected scholar Mahmood Mamdani argued along the same lines as Moyo and Yeros, hailing the *Third Chimurenga* as a successful NDR. This is how he put it:

> Zimbabwe has seen the greatest transfer of property in southern Africa since colonisation and it has all happened extremely rapidly. Eighty percent of the 4000 white farmers were expropriated; most of them stayed in Zimbabwe. Redistribution revolutionised property-holding, adding more than a hundred thousand small owners to the base of the property-pyramid. In social and economic – if not political – terms, this was a democratic revolution. But there was a heavy price to pay.[258]

While some left-nationalist scholars celebrated the situation in Zimbabwe as 'revolutionary,' those scholars concerned with human rights, democracy and good governance like Brian Raftopoulos, Ian Phimister and others saw the rise of an authoritarianism that was geared to abrogating every tenet of democracy.[259] Mahmood Mamdani's analysis of the Zimbabwean situation was even criticised by some left-leaning scholars like Horace Campbell and Patrick Bond, who failed to see any revolutionary potential in a partisan nation-state project that negatively affected peasants and workers.[260]

257. Ibid, p. 105.

258. M. Mamdani, 'Lessons of Zimbabwe,' in *London Review of Books*, 30 (23) (2008), p. 3.

259. B. Raftopoulos and I. Phimister, 'Zimbabwe Now: The Political Economy of Crisis and Coercion,' in *Historical Materialism*, 12 (4) 2004), pp. 355–82.

260. Responses to Mamdani's ideas were collated in a special issue of *ACAS Bulletin* of January 2009.

To the liberal scholars, the *Third Chimurenga* was a recipe for disorder that reflected the exhaustion of nationalism and the limits of neoliberalism. Raftopoulos openly criticised left-leaning scholars for ignoring the issues of human rights, democracy and good governance that were severely compromised during the *Third Chimurenga*.[261] He described Zimbabwean nationalism as an 'embattled' version that survived by attacking citizens. According to Raftopoulos, 'a particularly damaging feature of the ruling party's response to the crisis in Zimbabwe has been the state's overarching articulation of an intolerant, selective and racialised nationalist discourse.'[262] It became apparent from the debates that any nation-state project that failed to respect canons of democracy and human rights could hardly be considered progressive in the 21st century.

What was even more disturbing about the *Third Chimurenga* as a nation-state project was that it unfolded in tandem with the rapid descent of Zimbabwe as a promising transitional state with a robust economy into a condition of unprecedented crisis from the late 1990s, including the violence that ensued in the 2000s. It was during this period that the Zimbabwean nation-state project revealed all the symptoms of decadence that have been noticed in early decolonisers of the 1960s such as Ghana, Senegal and many others whose economy disintegrated in the 1970s. The intellectual debates on the Zimbabwean nation-state project also pitted the champions of national sovereignty and state nationalism against the advocates of liberal democracy, civil society, internationalism, human rights and good governance. This fault line was well captured by Mamdani:

> One group accuses the other of authoritarianism and self-righteous intolerance; it replies that its critics are wallowing in donor largesse. Nationalists speak of a historical racism that has merely migrated from government to civil society with the end of colonial rule, while civil society activists speak of an 'exhausted' nationalism, determined to feed old injustices.[263]

As the Zimbabwean nation-state project plunged deeper into economic, political and social crisis as well as conflict, the need to look back into the transformation of Zimbabwe from a colony into a sovereign nation became imperative. It became clear that though achievement of independence in 1980 was hailed and celebrated, the new republic was born in 1980 with a terrible defect, in that ethnic and racial issues remained active sources of conflict. When the land

261. B. Raftopoulos, 'The Zimbabwean Crisis and the Challenges for the Left,' in *Journal of Southern African Studies*, 32 (2) (June 2006), pp. 203–19.
262. B. Raftopoulos, 'Unreconciled Differences: The Limits of Reconciliation Politics in Zimbabwe,' in B. Raftopoulos and T. Savage (eds), *Zimbabwe: Injustice and Political Reconciliation* (Cape Town: Institute for Justice and Reconciliation, 2004), p. xiii.
263. Mamdani, 'Lessons of Zimbabwe,' p. 10.

question and the attendant racial politics re-emerged in more virulent character, it became evident that the Lancaster House Agreement of 1979 was nothing more than a 10-year armistice, in that it failed dismally to deal with the issue of land dispossession that had lain at the heart of the 'settler-native' conflicts since the 1890s.[264] The policy of reconciliation that Robert Mugabe proclaimed as a solution to the 'native-settler' conflict rang hollow without the resolution of the agrarian and national questions. This problem was well captured by Mamdani in these words:

> In the context of a former settler colony, a single citizenship for settlers and natives can only be the result of an overall metamorphosis whereby erstwhile colonisers and colonised are politically reborn as equal members of a single political community. The word reconciliation cannot capture this metamorphosis ... This is about establishing a political order based on consent and not conquest. It is about establishing a political community of equal and consenting citizens.[265]

Because the Lancaster House Settlement glossed over the core problem of 'settler-native' conflict, Zimbabwe found itself back to conflict at the beginning of 2000 that revolved around the question of land. No wonder then that race became the main trope, propelling a virulent and insurrectionist nationalism that became known as the *Third Chimurenga*.[266] However, the ZANU-PF attempts to project the *Third Chimurenga* as a progressive and redemptive nation-state project aimed at empowering peasants and a logical completing of the decolonisation process did not appeal to some constituencies within society. This was mainly due to the fact that ZANU-PF embarked on fast-track land reform at a time of election in 2000 and 2002. This time, ZANU-PF was facing a young but popular opposition party (MDC). The land reform was seen by many, particularly in opposition circles and civil society, as a political gimmick and as opportunistic tactic by ZANU-PF to win the peasant vote. Peasants had been hungry for land since 1980.

However, concentration on race as the driver of conflict in Zimbabwe tends to overshadow the issue of ethnicity, which has remained equally active in generating conflict since the split between ZAPU and ZANU in 1963. The apogee of ethnic conflict was the violence that engulfed Matabeleland and the Midlands from 1980 to 1987. Because of the 10-year Lancaster House armistice and the

264. B. Raftopoulos and T. Savage (eds), *Zimbabwe: Injustice and Political Reconciliation* (Cape Town: Institute for Justice and Reconciliation, 2004).

265. M. Mamdani, 'When Does a Settler Become a Native? Reflections on the Roots of Citizenship in Equatorial and South Africa' (Text of Inaugural Lecture delivered as A.C. Jordan Professor of African Studies, University of Cape Town, Wednesday, 13 May 1998).

266. R. Mugabe, *Inside the Third Chimurenga* (Harare: Government of Zimbabwe, 2001) and Donald S. Moore, *Suffering for Territory: Race, Place and Power in Zimbabwe* (Harare and New York: Weaver Press and Duke University Press, 2005).

policy of reconciliation, the race issue hibernated for some time as ethnicity occupied centre stage, with the ZANU-PF government using state institutions of violence to discipline and conquer a region considered to be a 'dissident' hotbed.[267] This region was inhabited by the minority Ndebele-speaking people who had supported PF-ZAPU under Joshua Nkomo. During the 1980s, ethnic-generated conflicts unfolded along the fault lines of Ndebele-Shona identities. Since the 1990s, the remnant of intra-Shona ethnicities also gradually came to the surface of national politics, further complicating the character of the Zimbabwean nation-state project. Beginning with factionalism in Masvingo province, whence such nationalist political heavyweights as Eddison Zvobgo and Simon Muzenda came, intra-Shona ethnicity reverberated loudly within ZANU-PF, creating various factions within the party. The zenith of this type of ethnicity was the Tsholotsho Declaration, which openly sought to accept the ubiquity of ethnicity as a challenge in Zimbabwean politics that needed to be addressed through careful balancing.[268]

What is clear from this case study of Zimbabwe is how difficult it is for a weak African state to pursue radical development in an environment dominated by neoliberal forces that are quick to discipline and decimate that which appears to deviate from neoliberal orthodoxy. At the same time, the crisis reflects the difficulties a state that squandered all chances to devise and implement sound economic and social policies in the 1980s and 1990s faces in placing the economy on a firm foundation to withstand global vicissitudes in the 2000s. At another level, the study indicates how a beleaguered nationalist leadership responded to international isolation through increasing repression at home, including militarisation of state institutions. It also indicates how difficult it is to try and resolve intractable economic justice issues without compromising ideals of democracy and human rights. What the Zimbabwean government managed to achieve, albeit in a problematic manner and at a terrible cost, was land redistribution. What spoiled this achievement was its entanglement with the politics of ZANU-PF regime security and the selfish primitive-accumulation instincts of government elites, which tended to amass land at the expense of landless peasants.

The Zimbabwe crisis reflects the tribulations that have haunted the broader African national project. Zimbabwe, just like many other postcolonial African

267. J. Alexander, J. McGregor and T. Ranger, *Violence and Memory: One Hundred Years in the 'Dark Forests' of Matabeleland* (Harare: Weaver Press, 2000) and Catholic Commission for Justice and Peace (CCJP) and Legal Resources Foundation (LRF), Breaking the Silence, *Building True Peace: Report on the Disturbances in Matabeleland and the Midlands, 1980–1988* (Harare: CCJP and LRF, 1997).

268. S.J. Ndlovu-Gatsheni, 'For the Nation to Live, the Tribe Must Die': The Politics of Ndebele Identity and Belonging in Zimbabwe,' in B. Zewde (ed.), *Society, State and Identity in African History* (Addis Ababa: Association of African Historians and Forum for Social Studies, 2008), pp. 167–99.

states, finds itself somewhere between the slow death of colonialism and the even slower birth of a sustainable African liberation ethos free from domination by hegemonic global powers. The struggle therefore needs to continue in the direction of the revival and renewal of the African project alongside intensification of regional integration founded on redemptive and people-centred pan-Africanism.

Bibliography

Ake, C., 2000, *The Feasibility of Democracy in Africa.* Dakar: CODESRIA.

Alexander, J., 2006, *The Unsettled Land: State-Making and the Politics of Land in Zimbabwe, 1893–2003.* London: James Currey.

Alexander, J., J. McGregor and T. Ranger, 2000, *Violence and Memory: OneHundred Years in the 'Dark Forests' of Matabeleland.* London: James Currey.

AMANI Trust, 2002, *Organised Violence and Torture in the June 2000 GeneralElection in Zimbabwe: A Report Prepared by the Mashonaland Programme of the AMANI Trust.* Harare: AMANI Trust, 28 February.

ANC,1979, 'African National Council: Aims and Objectives, Salisbury, 10 March1972', in Nyangoni, C. and G. Nyandoro (eds), *Zimbabwe Independence Movement.* London: R. Collings, p. 231.

Astrow, A., 1983, *Zimbabwe: A Revolution That Lost Its Way?* London: Zed Books.

Ayittey, G.B.N., 2005, *Africa Unchained: The Blueprint for Africa's Future.* New York: Palgrave Macmillan.

Bantu Mirror, 20 August 1960.

Bantu Mirror, 6 May 1961.

Beach, D.N.,1984, *Zimbabwe before 1900.* Gweru: Mambo Press.

—, 1994, *A Zimbabwean Past: Shona Dynastic Histories and Oral Traditions.* Gweru: Mambo Press.

—, 1994, *The Shona and Their Neighbours.* Oxford: Blackwell.

Bhebe, N., 1999, *The ZAPU and ZANU Guerrilla Warfare and the Evangelical Lutheran Church in Zimbabwe.* Gweru: Mambo Press.

—, 2004, *Simon Vengayi Muzenda and the Struggle for and Liberation of Zimbabwe.* Gweru: Mambo Press.

Billig, M.,1995, *Banal Nationalism.* London: Sage Publications.

Brumer, J., 1971, *For the President's Eyes Only.* Johannesburg: Hugh Keartland Publishers.

Catholic Commission for Justice and Peace (CCJP) and Legal Resources Foundation (LRF), 1997, *Breaking the Silence, Building True Peace: Report on the Disturbances in Matabeleland and the Midlands, 1980–1989.* Harare: CCJP and LRF.

Chambati, A., 1989, 'National Unity-ANC' in Banana, C.S. (ed.), *Zimbabwe, 1890–1990: Turmoil and Tenacity.* Harare: College Press: 147–59.

Chan, S., 2003, *Robert Mugabe: Life of Power and Violence.* London: I.B. Tauris.

Chanaiwa, D., 1981, 'Zimbabwe: Internal Settlement in Historical Perspective', in *Decolonisation of Africa: Southern Africa and the Horn of Africa.* New York: UNESCO.

Chen, K.H., 1998, 'Introduction: The Decolonisation Question,' in Chen, K.H. (ed.), *Trajectories: Inter-Asia Cultural Studies.* London: Routledge: 1–34.

Cheru, F., 2009, 'Development in Africa: The Imperial Project versus the National Project and the Need for Policy Space', *Review of African Political Economy*, 120: 275–8.

Chimhundu, H., 1992, 'Early Missionaries and the Ethnolinguistic Factor During the "Invention of Tribalism" in Zimbabwe', *Journal of African History*, 33(1):103–29.

Chipkin, I., 2007, *Do South African Exist? Nationalism, Democracy and the Identity of 'the People.'* Johannesburg: Wits University Press: 1–14.

The *Chronicle*, 25 January 1982.

Clapham, C., 1996, *Africa and the International System: The Politics of State Survival.* Cambridge: Cambridge University Press.

Davies, R., 2004, 'Memories of Underdevelopment: A Personal Interpretation ofZimbabwe's Economic Decline,' in Raftopoulos, B. and T. Savage (eds), *Zimbabwe: Injustice and Political Reconciliation.* Cape Town: Institute for Justice and Reconciliation, 19–41.

Doke, C.M., 1931, *A Comparative Study in Shona Phonetics.* Johannesburg: University of Witwatersrand Press.

—, 1931, *Report on the Unification of the Shona Dialects.* Hartford: Stephen Austin and Sons.

Dorman, S.R., 2001, 'Inclusion and Exclusion: NGOs and Politics in Zimbabwe.' Unpublished DPhil, University of Oxford.

Ekeh, P.P., 1975, 'Colonialism and the Two Publics in Africa: A Theoretical Statement', *Comparative Studies in Society and History*, 17(1):88–106.

FROLIZI, 1979, 'FROLIZI Draft Constitution', in Nyangoni, C. and G. Nyandoro (eds), *Zimbabwe Independence Movements*, p. 180.

Fukuyama, F., 1993, *The End of History and the Last Man.* New York: Harper Collins.

Hachipola, S.J., 1998, *A Survey of the Minority Languages of Zimbabwe.* Harare: University of Zimbabwe Publications.

Hammar, A. and B. Raftopoulos, 2003, 'Zimbabwe's Unfinished Business: Rethinking Land, State and Nation', in Hammar, A., B. Raftopoulos and S. Jensen (eds), *Zimbabwe's Unfinished Business: Rethinking Land, State and Nation in the Context of Crisis.* Harare: Weaver Press, 1–47.

Hardt, M. and T. Negri, 2000, *Empire.* Cambridge: Harvard University Press.

The Herald, 6 December 1997.

Higley, J., 1999, 'Transitions and Elites', in Braun, A. and Z. Barany (eds), *Dilemmas of Transition: The Hungarian Experience.* Boulder: Rowman and Littlefield: 38–58.

Jackson, R.H., 1990, *Quasi-States: Sovereignty, International Relations and the Third World.* Cambridge: Cambridge University Press.

Jeater, D., 2007, *Law, Language and Science: The Invention of the 'Native Mind' in Southern Rhodesia*, 1890–1930. Portsmouth NH: Heinemann.

Kaarsholm, K., 2006, 'Memoirs of a Dutiful Revolutionary: Fay Chung and the Legacies of the Zimbabwe Liberation War: An Introduction', in Chung, F., *Reliving the Second Chimurenga: Memories from the Liberation Struggle in Zimbabwe*. Uppsala: Nordic Africa Institute:1–18.

Laakso, L. and A.O. Olukoshi, 1996, 'The Crisis of the Post-Colonial Nation-State Project in Africa,' in Olukoshi, A.O. and L. Laakso (eds), *Challenges to the Nation-State in Africa*. Uppsala: Nordic Africa Institute: 11–12.

Libby, R.T., 1984, 'Development Strategies and Political Division within the Zimbabwean State', in Schartzberg , M. (ed.), *The Political Economy of Zimbabwe*. New York: Praeger.

Lindgren, B., 2005, 'The Politics of Identity and the Remembrance of Violence: Ethnicity and Gender at the Installation of a Female Chief in Zimbabwe', in Broch-Due, V. (ed.), *Violence and Belonging: The Quest for Identity in Post-Colonial Africa*. London and New York: Routledge.

Lonsdale, J., 1992, 'The Moral Economy of Mau Mau', in Berman, B. and J. Lonsdale (eds), *Unhappy Valley: Conflict in Kenya and Africa*. London: James Currey.

—, 2004, 'Moral and Political Argument in Kenya', in Bernam,B., D. Eyoh, and W. Kymlika (eds), *Ethnicity and Democracy in Africa*. Oxford: James Currey: 73–95.

Lun, D., 1985, *Guns and Rain: Guerrillas and Spirit Mediums in Zimbabwe*. Harare: Zimbabwe Publishing House.

Luxemburg, R., 1976, *The National Question*. New York: Monthly Review.

Makumbe, J., 2003, 'ZANU-PF: A Party in Transition?' in Cornwell, R. (ed.), *Zimbabwe's Turmoil: Problems and Prospects*. Pretoria: Institute for Security Studies: 24–38.

Mama, A., 2001, 'Challenging Subjects: Gender and Power in African Context', in Melber, H. (ed.), *Identity and Beyond: Rethinking Africanity*. Uppsala: Nordic Africa Institute: 1–20.

—, 2001, 'Challenging Subjects: Gender and Power in African Contexts', in H. Melber (ed.), *Identity and Beyond: Rethinking Africanity*. Uppsala: Nordiska Afrikaininstitute: 5–17.

Mamdani, M., 1996, *Citizen and Subject: Contemporary Africa and the Legacy of Late Colonialism*. Princeton NJ: Princeton University Press.

—, 1998, 'When Does a Settler Become a Native? Reflections on the Roots of Citizenship in Equatorial and South Africa.' Text of Inaugural Lecture delivered as A.C. Jordan Professor of African Studies, University of Cape Town, Wednesday, 13 May.

—, 2001, 'When Does a Settler Become a Native? Citizenship and Identity in a Settler Society', *Pretext: Literacy and Cultural Studies*, 10(1)(July):63–73.

—, 2001, *When Victims Become Killers: Colonialism, Nativism, and the Genocide in Rwanda*. Oxford: James Currey.

—, 2008, 'Lessons of Zimbabwe,' in *London Review of Books*, 30(23)(2008), p. 3.

Mandaza, I., 2007, 'Introduction: Edgar Tekere and Zimbabwe's Struggle for Independence', in Tekere, *Edgar 2-Boy Tekere*: 1–5.

Mandaza, I. and L. Sachikonye (eds), 1991, *The One Party State and Democracy: The Zimbabwe Debate*. Harare: SAPES Books.

Martin, D. and P. Johnson, 1981, *The Struggle for Zimbabwe: The Chimurenga War*. Harare: Zimbabwe Publishing House.

Mawema, M., 1979, 'Why I Resigned from the NDP to Join the Zimbabwe National Party, Salisbury 1961', in Nyangoni, C. and G. Nyandoro (eds), *Zimbabwe Independence Movements*, pp. 48–50.

Mazarire, G.C., 2009, 'Pre-Colonial Zimbabwe: Some Reflections', in Raftopoulos, B. and A.S. Mlambo (eds), *Becoming Zimbabwe: A History of Zimbabwe from Precolonial Times to 2008*. Harare: Weaver Press.

Mbeki, T., 2001, 'A Discussion Document: The Mbeki-Mugabe Papers: What Mbeki Told Mugabe' (August).

MDC, 2003, 'From Crisis to Democratic Human Centred Development', preface.

—, 2003, 'From Crisis to Democratic Human-Centred Development: Values, Goals and Polices of the Movement for Democratic Change (MDC)', December 2003.

—, 2000, *MDC Election Manifesto*.

—, 2005, *MDC Manifesto*.

—, 2007, 'A New Zimbabwe, A New Beginning'.

—, 2008, *MDC Manifesto*.

Meredith, M., 2002, *Our Votes, Our Guns: Robert Mugabe and the Tragedy of Zimbabwe*. New York: Public Affairs.

Miller, D., 2000, *Citizenship and National Identity*. Cambridge: Polity Press.

Mkandawire, T., 2002, 'From Liberation Movements to Governments: On Political Culture in Southern Africa', *African Sociological Review*, 6(1)(2002):12–13.

—, 2005, 'African Intellectuals and Nationalism,' in Mkandawire,T. (ed.), *African Intellectuals: Rethinking Politics, Language, Gender and Development*. London: Zed: 1–26.

Mombeshora, S., 1990, 'The Salience of Ethnicity in Political Development: The Case of Zimbabwe', *International Sociology*, 5(4):401–31.

Moore, D., 1991, 'The Ideological Formation of the Zimbabwean Ruling Class,' in *Journal of Southern African Studies*, 17(3)(September):472–95.

—, 1995, 'Democracy, Violence and Identity in the Zimbabwean War of Liberation: Reflections from the Realms of Dissent,' in *Canadian Journal of African Studies*, 29 (3) (December).

—, 1995, 'The Zimbabwe People's Army: Strategic Innovation or Moore of the Same? In N. Bhebe and T. Ranger (eds), *Soldiers in Zimbabwe's Liberation War*. London: James Currey, 1995: 73–103.

Moore, D.S., 2005, *Suffering for Territory: Race, Place and Power in Zimbabwe.* Harare and New York: Weaver Press and Duke University Press.

—, 2005, *Suffering for Territory: Race, Place, and Power in Zimbabwe.* Harare: Weaver Press.

Moto Magazine, 1 (4), August 1982, Moyo, J. 'Man of Truth: The Late Vice President Joseph Msika,' in http://www.newzimbabwe.com/blog/?p=665.

Moyo, S., J. Makumbe and B. Raftopoulos, 2000, *NGOs, the State and Politics in Zimbabwe.* Harare: SAPES.

Moyo, S. and P. Yeros, 2007, 'The Radicalised State: Zimbabwe's Interrupted Revolution,' *Review of African Political Economy*, 111:103–21.

Msindo, E., 2004, 'Ethnicity in Matabeleland, Zimbabwe: A Study of Kalanga–Ndebele Relations, 1860s-1980s.' Unpublished PhD thesis, University of Cambridge, August.

Mudenge, S.I.G., 1988, *A Political History of Munhumutapa.* Harare: Zimbabwe Publishing House.

Mufuka, K.M., 1979, 'Rhodesia's Internal Settlement: A Tragedy', *African Affairs,* 78(1979):439–40.

Mugabe, R.G., 2001, *Inside the Third Chimurenga.* Harare: Government of Zimbabwe.

Muzondidya, J. and S.J. Ndlovu-Gatsheni, 2007, 'Echoing Silences': Ethnicity in Post-Colonial Zimbabwe, 1980–2007,' *African Journal on Conflict Resolution,* 7(2):275–97.

Muzorewa, A.T., 1979, 'African National Council: Aims and Objectives, Salisbury, 10 March 1972', in Nyangoni, C. and G. Nyandoro (eds), *Zimbabwe Independence Movements*, p. 231.

—, 1979, 'African National Council: A Broadcast Appeal to Zimbabweans at Home and Abroad, Lusaka, Zambia, 19 March 1975', in Nyangoni, C. and G. Nyandoro (eds), *Zimbabwe Independence Movements*, p. 298.

—, 1979, *Rise up and Walk: An Autobiography.* London: Evans Brothers.

Ndhlovu, F., 2006, 'Gramsci, Doke and the Marginalisation of the Ndebele Language in Zimbabwe', *Journal of Multilingual and Multicultural Development*, 27(4):288–305.

Ndlovu-Gatsheni, S.J., 2006, 'Nationalist-Military Alliance and the Fate of Democracy in Zimbabwe', *African Journal on Conflict Resolution,* 6(1):49–80.

—, 2006, 'How Europe Ruled Africa: Matabeleland Region of Zimbabwe', *International Journal of Humanistic Studies*, 5:1–18.

—, 2006, 'Puppets or Patriots: A Study of Nationalist Rivalry Over the Spoils of Dying Settler Colonialism in Zimbabwe, 1977–1980', in Burszta, W.J., T. Kamusella, and S. Wojciechowski (eds), *Nationalisms Across the Globe: An Overview of Nationalism in State-Endowed and Stateless Nations: Volume II: The World.* Poznan: School of Humanities and Journalism: 345–97;

—, 2006, 'The Nativist Revolution and Development Conundrums in Zimbabwe,' *ACCORD Occasional Paper Series*, 1(4):1–40.

—, 2007, 'Re-Thinking the Colonial Encounter in Zimbabwe in the Early Twentieth Century,' *Journal of Southern African Studies*, 33(1)(March):173–91.

—, 2008, 'Black Republican Tradition, Nativism and Populist Politics in South Africa,' *Transformation: Critical Perspectives on Southern Africa*, 68:53–86.

—, 2008, 'Patriots, Puppets, Dissidents and the Politics of Inclusion and Exclusion in Contemporary Zimbabwe', *Eastern Africa Social Science Research Review*, XXIV (1) (January): 81–108.

—, 2008, 'For the Nation to Live, the Tribe Must Die': The Politics of Ndebele Identity and Belonging in Zimbabwe,' in Zewde, B. (ed.), *Society, State and Identity in African History*. Addis Ababa: Association of African Historians and Forum for Social Studies: 167–99

—, 2008, 'Reaping the Bitter Fruits of Stalinist Tendencies in Zimbabwe', *African Concerned Scholars Bulletin: Special Issue on the 2008 Zimbabwe Elections*, No. 79 (Spring): 21–31.

—, 2009, *Do 'Zimbabweans' Exist? Trajectories of Nationalism, National Identity Formation and Crisis in a Postcolonial State*. Oxford: Peter Lang AG International Academic Publishers.

—, 2009, 'Making Sense of Mugabeism in Local and Global Politics: 'So Blair Keep Your England and Let Me Keep My Zimbabwe,' *Third World Quarterly*, 30(6):1139–58.

Ngara, J. (1978). 'The Zimbabwe Revolution and the Internal Settlement', *Marxism Today* (November): 337–43.

Nkomo, J., 1979, 'The Case for Majority Rule in Rhodesia: Gonakudzingwa Camp, 1964', in Nyangoni, C. and G. Nyandoro (eds), *Zimbabwe Independence Movements*, p. 99.

Nkomo, J., 1984, *Nkomo: The Story of My Life*. London: Methuen.

Nyagumbo, M., 1981, *With the People: An Autobiography from the Zimbabwe Struggle*. London: Allison and Busby.

Nyangoni, C. and Nyandoro G. (eds), 1979, *Zimbabwe Independence Movements*. London: R. Collings.

Nyangoni, W.W., 1997, *African Nationalism in Zimbabwe (Rhodesia)*. Washington DC: University Press of America.

Osaghae, E.E., 2006, 'Colonialism and Civil Society in Africa: The Perspective of Ekeh's Two Publics', *Voluntas*, 17:205–35.

Prah, K.K., 2009, 'A Pan-Africanist Reflection: Point and Counterpoint.' Unpublished Paper, Centre for Advanced Studies of African Society (CASAS), University of Cape Town.

Raftopoulos, B., 2001, 'The Labour Movement and the Emergence of OppositionPolitics in Zimbabwe,' in Raftopoulos, B. and L. Sachikonye (eds),

Striking Back: The Labour Movement and the Post-Colonial State in Zimbabwe, 1980–2000. Harare: Weaver Press: 1–24.

—, 2004, 'Unreconciled Differences: The Limits of ReconciliationPolitics in Zimbabwe,' in Raftopoulos, B. and T. Savage (eds), *Zimbabwe: Injustice and Political Reconciliation*. Cape Town: Institute for Justice and Reconciliation.

—, 2006, 'The Zimbabwean Crisis and the Challenges for the Left,' *Journal of Southern African Studies*, 32(2)(June):203–19.

—, 2007, 'Nation, Race and History in Zimbabwean Politics,' in Dorman, S., D. Hammett, and P. Nugent (eds), *Making Nations, Creating Strangers: States and Citizenship in Africa*. Leiden and Boston: Brill: 181–94.

Raftopoulos, B. and I. Phimister, 2004, 'Zimbabwe Now: The Political Economy of Crisis and Coercion,' *Historical Materialism*, 12(4):355–82.

Ranger, T., 1967, *Revolt in Southern Rhodesia: A Study in African Resistance*. London: Heinemann.

—, 1980, 'The Changing of the Old Guard: Robert Mugabe and the Revival of ZANU,' *Journal of Southern African Studies*, 7(1)(October):71–90.

—, 1985, *Peasant Consciousness and Guerrilla War in Zimbabwe*. Harare: Zimbabwe Publishing House.

—, 1985, *The Creation of Tribalism in Zimbabwe*. Gweru: Mambo Press.

—, 1989, 'Missionaries, Migrants and the Manyika: The Invention of Ethnicity in Zimbabwe', in Leroy Vail (ed.), *The Creation of Tribalism in Southern Africa*. London: James Currey.

—, 1993, 'The Invention of Tradition Revisited: The Case of Colonial Africa', in Ranger, T. and O. Vaughan (eds), *Legitimacy and the State*, p. 63.

—, 1997, 'Leaving Africa: Making and Writing History of Zimbabwe.' Harare, Zimbabwe: Valedictory Lecture, Monomotapa, Monomotapa Crown Plaza, 19 June.

—, 1999, *Voices from the Rocks: Nature, Culture and History of the Matopos Hills of Zimbabwe*. Harare: Baobab.

—, 2004, 'Nationalist Historiography, Patriotic History and the History of the Nation: The Struggle Over the Past in Zimbabwe,' *Journal of Southern African Studies*, 30(2) (June):215–34.

Reed, W.C., 1993, 'International Politics and National Liberation: ZANU and the Politics of Contested Sovereignty in Zimbabwe', *African Studies Review*, 36(2) (September):31–59.

Reicher, S. and N. Hopkins, 2001, *Self and Nation: Categorisation, Contestation and Mobilisation*. London: SAGE Publications.

Rhodesian Government, 1978, *Rhodesian Constitutional Agreement, 3rd March 1978, No. 44*. Salisbury: Government Printer.

Roberts, R.S., 2005, 'Traditional Paramontcy and Modern Politics in Matabeleland: The End of the Lobengula Royal Family – and of Ndebele Particularism?', *Heritage of Zimbabwe,* 24:4–34.

Robin, S., 1996, 'Heroes, Heretics and Historians of the Zimbabwe Revolution: A Review Article of Norma Kriger's 'Peasant Voices' (1992),' *Zambezia* XXIII (i):31–74.

Rupiya, M., 2005, 'Zimbabwe: Governance through Military Operations,' *African Security Review,* 14(3):117–18.

Ruswa, G., 2009, 'Solving the Zimbabwean Crisis: A Reflection on Land Reform in the Context of Political Settlement.' Paper presented at the European Conference on African Studies of the Africa-Europe Group for Interdisciplinary Studies, Leipzig, Germany, 5 June.

Rutherford, B., 2001, *Working on the Margins: Black Workers, White Farmers in Postcolonial Zimbabwe.* London and Harare: Zed and Weaver Press.

—, 2007, 'Shifting Grounds in Zimbabwe: Citizenship and Farm Workers in the New Politics of Land, in Dorman, S., D. Hammett, and P. Nugent (eds), *Making Nations, Creating Strangers: State and Citizenship in Africa.* Leiden and Boston: Brill: 105–26.

Sachikonye, L., 1996, 'The National-State and Conflict in Zimbabwe', in Olukoshi, A.O. and L. Laakso (eds), *Challenges to the Nation-State in Africa.* Uppsala: Nordic Africa Institute: 138–52.

Said, E., 1993, *Culture and Imperialism.* London: Chatto and Windus.

Samkange, S., 1979, 'Statement of Appeal by Interim President Michael Mawema, Salisbury, 1960', in Nyangoni, C. and G. Nyandoro (eds), *Zimbabwe Independence Movements,* p. 21.

Samkange, S. and T.M. Samkange, 1980, *Hunhuism or Ubuntuism: A Zimbabwe Indigenous Political Philosophy.* Salisbury: Graham Publishing.

Saul, J.S., 2002, 'Starting from Scratch? A Reply to Jeremy Cronin', *Monthly Review,* 54(7):5–16.

—, 2008, *Decolonisation and Empire: Contesting the Rhetoric and Reality of Resurbordination in Southern Africa and Beyond.* Wales and Johannesburg: Merlin Press and Wits University Press.

Shamuyarira, N., 1979, 'Explanation of Why FROLIZI was formed', in Nyangoni, C. and G. Nyandoro (eds), *Zimbabwe Independence Movements,* pp. 171–2.

Shivji, I.G., 2003, 'The Rise, the Fall, and the Insurrection of Nationalism in Africa.' Paper presented as Keynote Address to CODESRIA East African Regional Conference, Addis Ababa, Ethiopia, 29–31 October.

Sibanda, E., 2005, *The Zimbabwe African People's Union, 1961–87: A Political History of Insurgency in Southern Rhodesia.* Trenton: Africa World Press.

Sithole, M., 1997, 'Zimbabwe's Eroding Authoritarianism', *Journal of Democracy,* 8(1):127–41.

—, 1999, *Zimbabwe: Struggles within the Struggle: Second Edition*. Harare: Rujeko Publishers.

—, 2001, 'Fighting Authoritarianism in Zimbabwe', *Journal of Democracy,* 12(1):56–79.

Sithole, N., 1959, *African Nationalism*. London: Oxford University Press.

—, 1968, *African Nationalism: Second Edition*. London: Oxford University Press.

—, 1970, *Roots of Revolution: Scenes from Zimbabwe*. Oxford: Oxford University Press.

—, 1978, *In Defence of the Rhodesian Constitutional Agreement: A Power Promise*. Salisbury: Graham Publishing.

—, 1979, 'On the Assassination of Herbert Chitepo and ZANU, 10 May 1976', in Nyangoni,C. and G. Nyandoro (eds), *Zimbabwe Independence Movements,* p. 310.

—, 1979, 'Presidential Address to the Inaugural Congress of Zimbabwe African National Union, Gwelo, 12–13 May 1964', in Nyangoni, C. and G. Nyandoro (eds), *Zimbabwe Independence Movements*: 75–85.

—, 1979, 'Zimbabwe African National Union: Presidential Address at the ZANU Inaugural Congress, Gwelo, 12–13 May 1964', in Nyangoni, C. and G. Nyandoro (eds), *Zimbabwe Independence Movements*, p. 75.

Smith-Hohn, J., 2009, 'Unpacking the Zimbabwe Crisis: A Situation Report,' *Institute for Security Studies Situation Report,* 10 September.

Southern Africa Report, 15(3)(June 2000).

Southern Rhodesia African National Congress, 1979, 'Statement of Principles, Policy and Programme, Salisbury 1957', in Nyangoni, C. and G. Nyandoro (eds), *Zimbabwe Independence Movements*, p. 3.

Southern Rhodesia, 1963, *Statute of Law of Southern Rhodesia: Volume 7*. Salisbury: Government Printer.

Sylvester, C., 1986, 'Zimbabwe's 1985 Elections: A Search for National Mythology', *Journal of Modern African Studies*, 24(1)(1986):246.

Tandon, Y., 2008, *Ending Aid Dependence*. Oxford: Fahamu Books.

Tekere, E., 2007, *Edgar 2-Boy Tekere: A Life in Struggle*. Harare: SAPES Books.

Tengende, N., 1994, 'Workers, Students and the Struggles for Democracy: State–Civil Society Relations in Zimbabwe.' Unpublished PhD thesis, Roskilde University.

Tshabangu, O.M., 1979, *The 11 March Movement in ZAPU-Revolution with the Revolution for Zimbabwe*. York: Tiger Papers Publications.

Tsvangirai, M., 2008, *Press Conference Statement,* 1 April.

Turino, T., 2000, *Nationalists, Cosmopolitans and Popular Music in Zimbabwe*. Chicago: Chicago University Press.

Verdery, K., 1996, 'Whither "Nation" and "Nationalism?"', in Balakrishnan, G. and B. Anderson (eds), *Mapping the Nation*. London and New York: Verso: 225–37.

Weinrich, A.K.H., 1973, *Black and White Elites in Rural Rhodesia*. Manchester: Manchester University Press.

West, M.O., 2002, *The Rise of an African Middle Class: Colonial Zimbabwe 1898–1965*. Bloomington: Indiana University Press.

White, L., 2003, *The Assassination of Herbert Chitepo: Text and Politics in Zimbabwe*. Bloomington and Indianapolis: Indiana University Press.

Windrich, E., 1975, *The Rhodesian Problem: A Documentary Record 1923–1973*. London and Boston: Routledge and Kegan Paul.

Yoshikuni, T., 2007, *African Urban Experiences in Colonial Zimbabwe: A Social History of Harare before 1925*. Harare: Weaver Press.

ZANU, 1966, 'ZANU in World Politics', *Zimbabwe Today*, 9 (18 April).

—, 1978, 'Diplomatic Struggle', *Zimbabwe News*, 10(6) (November-December).

—, 1979, 'Press Statement Issued by Supreme Council (Dare) on Behalf of Rev. N. Sithole, ZANU President, Lusaka, 19 April 1971,' in Nyangoni, C. and G. Nyandoro (eds), *Zimbabwe Independence Movements*, p. 170.

ZAPU, 1968, *Confidential Draft Constitution of the Zimbabwe African People's Union* (Lusaka).

ZAPU, 1979, 'Policy Statement, Salisbury, 21 August 1963', in Nyangoni, C. and G. Nyandoro (eds), *Zimbabwe Independence Movements*, p. 65.

Zeleza, P.T., 2003, *Rethinking Africa's 'Globalisation' Volume 1: The Intellectual Challenges*. Trenton: Africa World Press.

—, 2003, 'Pan-Africanism' in Zeleza, P.T. and D. Eyoh (eds), *Encyclopaedia of Twentieth Century African History*. London and New York: Routledge: 415–18.

—, 2006, Imagining and Inventing the Postcolonial State in Africa,' *Contours: A Journal of African Diaspora* in http://www.press.uillionnois.edu/journal/contours/1.1/zeleza.html

Zimbabwe Human Rights NGO Forum, 2001, *Politically Motivated Violence in Zimbabwe 2000–2001: A Report on the Campaign of Political Repression Conducted by the Zimbabwean Government Under the Guise of Carrying Out Land Reform*. Harare: Zimbabwe Human Rights NGO Forum, August.

Zimbabwe Times: A Journal of the Zimbabwe African National Union, September 1976, 1–6.

Zimbabwe Times, 28 March 1978.

DISCUSSION PAPERS PUBLISHED BY THE INSTITUTE

Recent issues in the series are available electronically for download free of charge
www.nai.uu.se

1. Kenneth Hermele and Bertil Odén, *Sanctions and Dilemmas. Some Implications of Economic Sanctions against South Africa.*
   1988. 43 pp. ISBN 91-7106-286-6
2. Elling Njål Tjönneland, *Pax Pretoriana. The Fall of Apartheid and the Politics of Regional Destabilisation.*
   1989. 31 pp. ISBN 91-7106-292-0
3. Hans Gustafsson, Bertil Odén and Andreas Tegen, *South African Minerals. An Analysis of Western Dependence.*
   1990. 47 pp. ISBN 91-7106-307-2
4. Bertil Egerö, *South African Bantustans. From Dumping Grounds to Battlefronts.*
   1991. 46 pp. ISBN 91-7106-315-3
5. Carlos Lopes, *Enough is Enough! For an Alternative Diagnosis of the African Crisis.*
   1994. 38 pp. ISBN 91-7106-347-1
6. Annika Dahlberg, *Contesting Views and Changing Paradigms.*
   1994. 59 pp. ISBN 91-7106-357-9
7. Bertil Odén, *Southern African Futures. Critical Factors for Regional Development in Southern Africa.*
   1996. 35 pp. ISBN 91-7106-392-7
8. Colin Leys and Mahmood Mamdani, *Crisis and Reconstruction – African Perspectives.*
   1997. 26 pp. ISBN 91-7106-417-6
9. Gudrun Dahl, *Responsibility and Partnership in Swedish Aid Discourse.*
   2001. 30 pp. ISBN 91-7106-473-7
10. Henning Melber and Christopher Saunders, *Transition in Southern Africa – Comparative Aspects.*
    2001. 28 pp. ISBN 91-7106-480-X
11. *Regionalism and Regional Integration in Africa.*
    2001. 74 pp. ISBN 91-7106-484-2
12. Souleymane Bachir Diagne, et al., *Identity and Beyond: Rethinking Africanity.*
    2001. 33 pp. ISBN 91-7106-487-7
13. Georges Nzongola-Ntalaja, et al., *Africa in the New Millennium.* Edited by Raymond Suttner.
    2001. 53 pp. ISBN 91-7106-488-5
14. *Zimbabwe's Presidential Elections 2002.* Edited by Henning Melber.
    2002. 88 pp. ISBN 91-7106-490-7
15. Birgit Brock-Utne, *Language, Education and Democracy in Africa.*
    2002. 47 pp. ISBN 91-7106-491-5
16. Henning Melber et al., *The New Partnership for Africa's development (NEPAD).*
    2002. 36 pp. ISBN 91-7106-492-3
17. Juma Okuku, *Ethnicity, State Power and the Democratisation Process in Uganda.*
    2002. 42 pp. ISBN 91-7106-493-1
18. Yul Derek Davids, et al., *Measuring Democracy and Human Rights in Southern Africa.* Compiled by Henning Melber.
    2002. 50 pp. ISBN 91-7106-497-4
19. Michael Neocosmos, Raymond Suttner and Ian Taylor, *Political Cultures in Democratic South Africa.* Compiled by Henning Melber.
    2002. 52 pp. ISBN 91-7106-498-2
20. Martin Legassick, *Armed Struggle and Democracy. The Case of South Africa.*
    2002. 53 pp. ISBN 91-7106-504-0
21. Reinhart Kössler, Henning Melber and Per Strand, *Development from Below. A Namibian-Case Study.*
    2003. 32 pp. ISBN 91-7106-507-5
22. Fred Hendricks, *Fault-Lines in South African Democracy. Continuing Crises of Inequality and Injustice.*
    2003. 32 pp. ISBN 91-7106-508-3
23. Kenneth Good, *Bushmen and Diamonds. (Un) Civil Society in Botswana.*
    2003. 39 pp. ISBN 91-7106-520-2
24. Robert Kappel, Andreas Mehler, Henning Melber and Anders Danielson, *Structural Stability in an African Context.*
    2003. 55 pp. ISBN 91-7106-521-0
25. Patrick Bond, *South Africa and Global Apartheid. Continental and International Policies and Politics.*
    2004. 45 pp. ISBN 91-7106-523-7
26. Bonnie Campbell (ed.), *Regulating Mining in Africa. For whose benefit?*
    2004. 89 pp. ISBN 91-7106-527-X
27. Suzanne Dansereau and Mario Zamponi, *Zimbabwe – The Political Economy of Decline.* Compiled by Henning Melber.
    2005. 43 pp. ISBN 91-7106-541-5

28. Lars Buur and Helene Maria Kyed, *State Recog-ni-tion of Traditional Authority in Mozambique. The nexus of Community Representation and State Assist-ance.*
 2005. 30 pp. ISBN 91-7106-547-4
29. Hans Eriksson and Björn Hagströmer, *Chad – Towards Democratisation or Petro-Dictatorship?*
 2005. 82 pp.ISBN 91-7106-549-
30. Mai Palmberg and Ranka Primorac (eds), *Skin-ning the Skunk – Facing Zimbabwean Futures.*
 2005. 40 pp. ISBN 91-7106-552-0
31. Michael Brüntrup, Henning Melber and Ian Taylor, *Africa, Regional Cooperation and the World Market – Socio-Economic Strategies in Times of Global Trade Regimes.* Com-piled by Henning Melber.
 2006. 70 pp. ISBN 91-7106-559-8
32. Fibian Kavulani Lukalo, *Extended Handshake or Wrestling Match? – Youth and Urban Culture Celebrating Politics in Kenya.*
 2006.58 pp. ISBN 91-7106-567-9
33. Tekeste Negash, *Education in Ethiopia: From Crisis to the Brink of Collapse.*
 2006. 55 pp. ISBN 91-7106-576-8
34. Fredrik Söderbaum and Ian Taylor (eds) *Micro-Regionalism in West Africa. Evidence from Two Case Studies.*
 2006. 32 pp. ISBN 91-7106-584-9
35. Henning Melber (ed.), *On Africa – Scholars and African Studies.*
 2006. 68 pp. ISBN 978-91-7106-585-8
36. Amadu Sesay, *Does One Size Fit All? The Sierra Leone Truth and Reconciliation Commission Revisited.*
 2007. 56 pp. ISBN 978-91-7106-586-5
37. Karolina Hulterström, Amin Y. Kamete and Henning Melber, *Political Opposition in African Countries – The Case of Kenya, Namibia, Zambia and Zimbabwe.*
 2007. 86 pp. ISBN 978-7106-587-2
38. Henning Melber (ed.), *Governance and State Delivery in Southern Africa. Examples from Bot-swana, Namibia and Zimbabwe.*
 2007. 65 pp. ISBN 978-91-7106-587-2
39. Cyril Obi (ed.), *Perspectives on Côte d'Ivoire: Between Political Breakdown and Post-Conflict Peace.*
 2007. 66 pp. ISBN 978-91-7106-606-6
40. Anna Chitando, *Imagining a Peaceful Society. A Vision of Children's Literature in a Post-Conflict Zimbabwe.*
 2008. 26 pp. ISBN 978-91-7106-623-7
41. Olawale Ismail, *The Dynamics of Post-Conflict Reconstruction and Peace Building in West Africa. Between Change and Stability.*
 2009.52 pp. ISBN 978-91-7106-637-4
42. Ron Sandrey and Hannah Edinger, *Examining the South Africa–China Agricultural Relationship.*
 2009. 58 pp. ISBN 978-91-7106-643-5
43. Xuan Gao, *The Proliferation of Anti-Dumping and Poor Governance in Emerging Economies.*
 2009. 41 pp. ISBN 978-91-7106-644-2
44. Lawal Mohammed Marafa, *Africa's Business and Development Relationship with China. Seeking Moral and Capital Values of the Last Economic Frontier.*
 2009. xx pp. ISBN 978-91-7106-645-9
45. Mwangi wa Githinji, *Is That a Dragon or an Elephant on Your Ladder? The Potential Impact of China and India on Export Led Growth in Afri-can Countries.*
 2009. 40 pp. ISBN 978-91-7106-646-6
46. Jo-Ansie van Wyk, *Cadres, Capitalists, Elites and Coalitions. The ANC, Business and Development in South Africa.*
 2009. 61 pp. ISBN 978-91-7106-656-5
47. Elias Courson, *Movement for the Emancipation of the Niger Delta (MEND). Political Marginaliza-tion, Repression and Petro-Insurgency in the Niger Delta.*2009. 30 pp. ISBN 978-91-7106-657-2
48. Babatunde Ahonsi, *Gender Violence and HIV/AIDS in Post-Conflict West Africa. Issues and Responses.* 2010.
 38 pp. ISBN 978-91-7106-665-7
49. Usman Tar and Abba Gana Shettima, *Endan-gered Democracy? The Struggle over Secularism and its Implications for Politics and Democracy in Nigeria.*
 2010. 21 pp. ISBN 978-91-7106-666-4
50. Garth Andrew Myers, *Seven Themes in African Urban Dynamics.*2010. 28 pp.
 ISBN 978-91-7106-677-0
51. Abdoumaliq Simone, *The Social Infrastructures of City Life in Contemporary Africa.*
 2010. 33 pp. ISBN 978-91-7106-678-7
52. Li Anshan, *Chinese Medical Cooperation in Af-rica. With Special Emphasis on the Medical Teams and Anti-Malaria Campaign.*
 2011. 24 pp. ISBN 978-91-7106-683-1
53. Folashade Hunsu, *Zangbeto: Navigating the Spaces Between Oral art, Communal Security And Conflict Mediation in Badagry, Nigeria.*
 2011. 27 pp. ISBN 978-91-7106-688-6

54. Jeremiah O. Arowosegbe, *Reflections on the Challenge of Reconstructing Post-Conflict States in West Africa: Insights from Claude Ake's Political Writings.*
2011. 40 pp. ISBN 978-91-7106-689-3

55. Bertil Odén, *The Africa Policies of Nordic Countries and the Erosion of the Nordic Aid Model: A comparative study.*
2011. 66 pp. ISBN 978-91-7106-691-6

56. Angela Meyer, P*eace and Security Cooperation in Central Africa: Developments, Challenges and Prospects.*
2011. 47 pp ISBN 978-91-7106-693-0

57. Godwin R. Murunga, *Spontaneous or Premeditated? Post-Election Violence in Kenya.*
2011. 58 pp. ISBN 978-91-7106-694-7

58. David Sebudubudu & Patrick Molutsi, *The Elite as a Critical Factor in National Development: The Case of Botswana.*
2011. 48 pp. ISBN 978-91-7106-695-4

59. Sabelo J. Ndlovu-Gatsheni, *The Zimbabwean Nation-State Project. A Historical Diagnosis of Identity and Power-Based Conflicts in a Postcolonial State.*
2011. 97 pp. ISBN 978-91-7106-696-1

www.ingramcontent.com/pod-product-compliance
Ingram Content Group UK Ltd.
Pitfield, Milton Keynes, MK11 3LW, UK
UKHW061827190726
13853UKWH00009B/2473